FROM
MOTHER
TO
MOTHER

FROM
MOTHER
TO
MOTHER

Recipes from a family kitchen

LISA FAULKNER

SIMON &
SCHUSTER

London · New York · Sydney · Toronto · New Delhi

A CBS COMPANY

Contents

* * * * * * *

.

I believe that most of us cook and create by being given nuggets of inspiration. We take recipes and cook from them, then we cook them again, and tweak them and add things, and then we cook them again. It was this idea of passing on favourite dishes to the next generation that inspired my first book, *Recipes from my Mother for my Daughter*. My grandmother's best friend's recipes became my mother's recipes, which in turn became mine and my sister's, and will, I hope, one day become my daughter's. That to me is the joy of cooking. It is sharing a love of food, a memory of why something tasted so good, or simply of wanting to feed your loved ones.

For so long, my professional life was defined by acting. But over the last few years, I've had the chance to add to this, to be thought of as a 'cook' too. This transition has been wonderful and it is a privilege to be able to share and pass on recipes to readers through cooking on television and writing my recipe books.

The other major thing that defines me is being a mother. Motherhood, as many of you know, didn't come easily to me, but when it finally did, it brought with it new rollercoasters, dramas and miracles and my life since then has felt complete. Losing my own precious, wonderful mummy at the age of 16 was the hardest thing that has happened to me. Not a day goes by when I don't think of her and love her and talk about her as if she were still here... And before my own beautiful daughter came along and I became a mother myself, it was my mother's death that also defined me. Those 16 years with her shaped me and taught me how to be a mum myself.

This got me thinking about mothers and the pride and sense of responsibility and achievement I feel every day and how very important this role is. The chance to nurture and to nourish means the world to me, as it does to almost every mother out there, and I wanted to celebrate that privilege. This book is the result. It started life as an email that I wrote to my family and friends, and friends of friends who are mothers. I asked them what they liked to cook and eat: what their favourite fallbacks are, their comfort dishes, the meals they make for their families when time is short.

The recipes that follow were inspired by their replies. I have tweaked, rewritten, added and played around with their ideas, and added my own family's staples. But without my friends' willingness to share their treasured favourites, there would be no book. So to all the mothers who contributed, I am eternally grateful and these recipes are dedicated to you.

I believe this is how all good books come together. I believe this is how all good things come together: by sharing and loving and giving unconditionally. You could also say that is the definition of a mother.

In a world that is ever changing and not always a smooth ride, food is a thing that binds us.

So here are those treasures, from mother to mother, with all my love and gratitude...

POULTRY

* * * * * *

Auntie Lil's Chicken Soup

Chicken Fiesta

Chicken and Kale Bake

Fern's Jubbly Pie

Spiced Chicken Bread Bowls

Chicken with Tarragon and Peppers

Red Chicken

Nina's Chicken Parcels

Roast Chicken with Creamy Herb Stuffing

Chicken Satay Balls

Chicken, Pea and Pancetta Bake

Dhruv's Mum's Easy Chicken Curry

Turkey Schnitzel and Chik Chak Salad

Clementine's Red Duck Curry

Cheat's Crispy Duck and Pancakes

Auntie Lil's Chicken Soup

Juliet is Jewish and almost every Friday her family starts celebrating Shabbat with its version of this chicken soup, which has been passed down through generations. Famously known as 'Jewish penicillin', a chicken soup is thought to cure all kinds of ailments, and at the age of 96 Juliet's grandma Molly is still making hers. Juliet shared her sister's (Auntie Lil's) recipe with me and I now use it whenever my daughter Billie, or anyone in our family is feeling under the weather. The recipe has quite a few steps, so it's a little bit of labour of love, but it's definitely worth the effort! It freezes beautifully and I've come to love it so much that I make big batches so I always have an emergency stock in the freezer. I feel very honoured that such a treasure has been shared with me and now with you.

Serves 6-8

10-12 chicken wings
8 carrots, chopped
4 celery sticks, chopped
1 onion, skin on, quartered
handful of flat-leaf
  parsley
1 bay leaf
1 heaped tsp Marmite
1 chicken stock cube
12 black peppercorns
1 tbsp caster sugar
1 lemon wedge
200g vermicelli noodles,
  roughly crushed

Place all the ingredients except the sugar, lemon wedge and noodles in a very large pan and cover with about 3 litres of water. Bring to the boil and remove the scum with a slotted spoon. Simmer over a low heat for 1½-2 hours. Remove from the heat and leave to rest overnight in the fridge.

The next morning, scoop off the fat. Place the pan back on a medium-low heat. Add the sugar and heat the soup through thoroughly. Check the seasoning and add a squeeze of lemon, if necessary.

Stir all the ingredients and bash the chicken wings around. Remove from the heat, allow to cool, then strain, reserving some of the vegetables and taking the meat off the chicken wings - set these aside until ready to serve.

Place the soup in the fridge: it should become jelly-like and the fat will rise to the surface. Spoon off the fat and discard.

Reheat the soup over a low heat, adding the reserved chicken and vegetables until heated through, then add the noodles for 2-3 minutes, until cooked, check the seasoning and serve.

Chicken Fiesta

I hate gyms. I like exercise that is disguised, such as a long, brisk walk! My friend Candy is a busy mother of three boys but every week we meet up to walk with my sister and our friend Frances. We walk and chat, give each other advice and support and, most importantly, swap recipes. Candy likes this recipe because it can all be prepared in advance. It was originally a recipe from her son's home economics class that she has adapted and now it's a firm favourite in her household.

Serves 4-6

I tbsp olive oil
150g cooking chorizo,
   sliced
I onion, finely chopped
2 celery sticks, finely
   chopped
I red pepper, thinly sliced
3 garlic cloves, crushed
500g boneless, skinless
   chicken thighs, roughly
   chopped
I x 400g tin chopped
   tomatoes
I tbsp tomato purée
250g basmati rice
600ml chicken stock
small bunch of oregano,
   chopped
handful of chopped
   flat-leaf parsley
salt and pepper

Heat the oil in a lidded ovenproof pan or casserole dish and cook the chorizo for 5 minutes over a high heat until it releases its lovely paprika oils. Add the onion, celery and pepper, reduce the heat to medium and cook for a further 10 minutes. Then add the garlic and cook for 30 seconds, followed by the chicken, tomatoes and tomato purée. Season well.

Heat the oven to 190°C/gas 5. Add the rice, stock and oregano to the pan, stir to combine, then bring to the boil. Cover and cook in the oven for 25-30 minutes, stirring once after about 15 minutes. Remove from the oven, stir through the parsley and serve.

Chicken and Kale Bake

In her own words, my Auntie Susan is a 'lazy cook'. She also claims she isn't a very good cook but I disagree and love all her food. This dish comes from a time when we all had lots of tins in our cupboards in preparation for a catastrophe. I know that making a sauce from a soup might sound a bit outdated or weird, but as a shortcut to flavour, I promise you it works; it's super quick and very tasty.

Serves 4

I tbsp olive oil
4 chicken breasts, cut into
   bite-sized pieces
300g kale or cavolo nero
I x 400g tin Campbell's
   Condensed Cream of
   Chicken soup
I00g crème fraîche
I tsp curry powder
I tsp lemon juice
handful of panko or fresh
   breadcrumbs
salt and pepper

Heat the oil in a non-stick frying pan. Season the chicken then cook over a high heat until coloured all over. Tip into an ovenproof dish, about 25 x 20cm.

Bring a pan of water to the boil and blanch the kale for a couple of minutes, then drain and add to the chicken.

Heat the oven to 180°C/gas 4. In a bowl, combine the soup, crème fraîche, curry powder and lemon juice. Pour over the chicken and kale and mix well, then scatter the breadcrumbs over the top. Bake for 15–20 minutes until golden brown and bubbling.

Fern's Jubbly Pie

During my dark days of trying to become a mum, my lovely friend Fern Britton really helped me. I was invited to appear on *This Morning* to talk about a show I was doing and fertility expert Zita West was one of the other guests. Fern knew I was struggling to get pregnant so she had a word with Zita and told me I could have a chat with her after the show - Fern has a heart of gold. When her four children were little, Fern would make them her 'jubbly pie', her clever way of getting them to eat their veg without noticing. Fern would purée all her veg so that they were completely hidden from fussy eaters, but I like the textures they give the pie, and my family are happy to eat them so I just leave them as they are.

Serves 4-6

800g floury potatoes, peeled
   and cubed
2 tbsp vegetable oil
I onion, finely chopped
I leek, finely chopped
300g minced turkey or
   chicken
50g frozen peas
I small carrot, finely
   chopped
I celery stick, finely
   chopped
2 tbsp plain flour
6 tbsp tomato ketchup
I50ml chicken stock
good knob of unsalted
   butter, plus extra to
   dot over
splash of milk
salt and pepper

Put the potatoes into a large pan of cold salted water, bring to the boil and simmer for 15-20 minutes until really tender.

Meanwhile, heat the oil in a frying pan, add the onion and leek and cook for 5 minutes to soften. Add the minced turkey or chicken, peas, carrots and celery and cook for a further 10 minutes. Add the flour and ketchup and mix well, then pour in the stock and bring to the boil, stirring all the time. Cook for 10 minutes or until the vegetables are cooked through.

Drain and mash the potatoes with the butter and a splash of milk. Season well.

Heat the oven to 220°C/gas 7. Place a layer of potato in the bottom of an ovenproof dish, about 25 x 20cm. Top with some of the mince and vegetable mixture, then repeat the layering until the dish is full, finishing with a topping of potato. Dot the potato with butter and place in the oven. Cook for 25 minutes until the top is nicely browned and crunchy.

Spiced Chicken Bread Bowls

Like so many mums, I struggle to think what to cook for my family every day that is tasty, nourishing and different to what we ate last week! Billie loves chicken pie and chicken curry, so this is a sort of mash-up of the two. The scooped-out bread rolls are just a fun idea instead of pastry, and children like the novelty value of being able to eat their bowl.

Serves 4-8 (depending on how hungry you are)

30g unsalted butter
I onion, finely chopped
2 tsp mild curry powder
30g plain flour
I-2 tbsp tomato purée
250-300ml chicken stock
I50g frozen peas
4 cooked chicken breasts, chopped
4 tbsp crème fraîche
8 crusty bread rolls
salt and pepper

Melt the butter in a frying pan and fry the onions gently over a low heat until softened. Stir through the curry powder and cook for 1 minute. Add the flour and cook for another minute or so. Add the tomato purée, chicken stock and peas and allow to bubble away until the sauce thickens. Remove from the heat and leave to cool.

Heat the oven to 180°C/gas 4. Stir the chicken and crème fraîche into the mixture and season to taste. Cut the tops off the rolls and scoop out the insides (keep them to use as breadcrumbs), then fill the rolls with the chicken mix and bake for 10–12 minutes, until the rolls are golden on the outside and the chicken is piping hot.

Chicken with Tarragon and Peppers

This recipe was given to me by my work colleague, Jay. She had a copy of my first book but it was eaten by their puppy, and Jay's husband called me to say that she really loved the book and asked whether I could sign a copy of a new one. I was really flattered that she liked it that much, so asked her what her own go-to recipe was. This recipe was her mum's and what's great about it is that it works just as well on a weeknight family table as for a Saturday night dinner party.

Serves 4

2 tbsp olive oil
I large onion, finely sliced
I x 190g jar of roasted red
  peppers, drained and
  sliced
30g unsalted butter
4 chicken breasts, skin on
300ml dry white wine
I tsp tarragon vinegar
I x 400g tin plum tomatoes
good pinch of sugar
3 tarragon stalks, plus I-2
  tbsp chopped tarragon
  leaves
300g crème fraîche
salt and pepper
plain boiled rice, to serve

Heat the oil in a pan and gently fry the onion over a low heat for 5 minutes until softened. Add the peppers and cook for 2 minutes, then add the butter and heat until foaming. Add the chicken, skin-side down and leave it to brown – about 6 minutes, then flip the breasts over. Add the wine and vinegar and allow to bubble for about 3 minutes, then add the tomatoes, sugar, tarragon and seasoning and leave to simmer for 15 minutes.

Stir through the crème fraîche and chopped tarragon and cook for a further few minutes, until the sauce is bubbling well. Serve it simply with the plain boiled rice.

Red Chicken

My friend Jason remembers his mum making this for him as a child, and whenever he goes home to see her he asks for 'red chicken'. It's such a great quick dinner for families. Everything is bunged in a freezer bag and left to marinate, so you can start it in the morning and come home to a dinner that just needs to be thrown into the oven and served with rice, pasta or mash.

Serves 4-6

I onion, sliced
IOOg sundried tomatoes,
   chopped
200g passata
handful of basil leaves,
   plus extra to serve
200ml red wine
I garlic clove, smashed
2 tbsp olive oil
IOOml chicken stock
6 chicken thighs, skin on
salt and pepper

In a large freezer bag, combine all the ingredients except the chicken and season well. Add the chicken and massage the marinade all over. Leave to marinate for a few hours or overnight.

Heat the oven to 180°C/gas 4. Transfer the marinated chicken to a shallow ovenproof dish and bake for 30-40 minutes until the skin is crispy and the sauce is bubbling. Tear over a little extra basil for a hit of freshness and specks of green.

Nina's Chicken Parcels

My godmother Nina was one of my mum's best friends. She has looked after me and my sister ever since our mum died and I love her so very dearly. She is also a great cook and we spend lots of time talking about food. The selection of veg inside these parcels is lovely and summery, but you could switch them up according to what's available at the time of year. Serve with rice or boiled potatoes.

Serves 4

4 handfuls of spinach
16 asparagus spears
4 skinless chicken breasts
150g Boursin cheese
270g cherry tomatoes
butter
4 tbsp double cream
120ml chicken stock
1 lemon
4 tbsp finely chopped
  flat-leaf parsley
salt and pepper

Heat the oven to 190°C/gas 5. Take 4 large pieces of non-stick baking paper and divide the spinach and asparagus between them, then top with a chicken breast. Spread the Boursin over each chicken breast, dividing it equally, then add the tomatoes, a knob of butter, a tablespoon of cream and 2 tablespoons of chicken stock, a squeeze of lemon juice and a tablespoon of parsley to each. Season with salt and plenty of pepper.

Bring the edges of the baking paper up around the chicken to form 4 loose-fitting parcels and seal the edges tightly. Place the parcels on a baking tray in the oven for 30 minutes.

Pop each parcel on to a plate and allow people to open them at the table. In Nina's words: 'Surprise, surprise!'

Roast Chicken with Creamy Herb Stuffing

Billie is the same age as my colleague and friend Nicola's daughter, so we have spent a lot of time discussing school, mood swings and activities. Since we met, Nicola has been promising to make me Sunday lunch and serve me her signature roast chicken. We haven't quite managed it yet, but in the meantime, she's shared her delicious recipe. I know a lot of people don't like goat's cheese, but I promise that if you use a really soft one like Chavroux, it doesn't have too strong a flavour and just tastes beautiful mixed with the herbs and other stuffing ingredients. If you're still not converted you could substitute ricotta.

Serves 4

150g soft goat's cheese
(I use Chavroux)
large handful of herbs
(tarragon, parsley, thyme),
finely chopped
grated zest and juice of
1 lemon
1 anchovy fillet, finely
chopped
1 garlic clove, crushed
1 x 1.2kg whole chicken
3 peppers, red and yellow,
finely sliced
200g vine tomatoes,
quartered
olive oil
200ml dry white wine
salt and pepper

Heat the oven to 200°C/gas 6. In a bowl, mix the goat's cheese with the herbs, lemon zest, anchovy and garlic and season well. Separate the skin from the chicken using your fingers, sliding them up under the neck end and gently easing the skin away from the breast. Push the goat's cheese mixture up under the skin of the chicken, using your fingers to spread it evenly.

Put the peppers and tomatoes into a large roasting tin, season and drizzle with oil, then place the chicken on top. Pour the lemon juice over the chicken and roast it for 30 minutes, then pour in the white wine and continue to roast for a further 30 minutes until the chicken is golden and cooked through - stick a skewer into a thigh; the juices should run clear.

Transfer the chicken to a warmed serving plate and rest for at least 10 minutes. Spoon the roasted vegetables around the chicken and serve.

Chicken Satay Balls

My other half, John, is a chef and an Aussie. Ever since he came back from working in Malaysia and made this dish for Billie and me I have been pestering him for the recipe. A traditional satay sauce is quite thick, but for this dish John loosens it with coconut milk to make a more liquid sauce for the chicken balls and noodles. I don't think you will ever want to buy a jar of ready-made satay sauce again, but for those among you who have no time but want to make the balls and noodles, you can cheat and use shop-bought sauce and then loosen it with coconut milk, I won't tell!

If your children are reluctant to try spice, satay is a great way to introduce them to it gently. There's only a mild hit of chilli, and most kids just love the sweetness of the peanut butter mixed with the coconut milk – which is seriously moreish – so they don't even notice there's a bit of kick behind them.

Serves 4

1 x 400g tin coconut milk,
  chilled for a few hours
  or overnight
2 tsp Thai red curry paste
3 tbsp peanut butter
2 tsp light soy sauce
400g minced chicken or
  turkey
200g medium egg noodles

To serve
1 tbsp toasted sesame seeds
4 spring onions, finely
  sliced
handful of chopped
  coriander
lime wedges

Without shaking the tin of coconut milk, open and scoop the solid layer of cream from the top into a pan. Add the curry paste and cook over a medium–high heat until the sauce splits. Add the peanut butter and soy sauce and a third of the remaining coconut milk, mix together then bring to the boil and bubble away until thickened. Keep the sauce warm over a low heat while you make the chicken balls.

Add a heaped tablespoon of this sauce to the minced chicken, stir to combine, and shape into balls – about the size of a ping pong ball. Heat a frying pan and brown the chicken balls all over, then add them to the sauce with the remaining coconut milk.

Cook the noodles according to the packet instructions, then drain and add to the chicken balls and sauce. Toss everything together then serve scattered with the sesame seeds, spring onions, coriander and lime wedges to squeeze over.

Chicken, Pea and Pancetta Bake

My mum was a big fan of one-pot dishes and I am too. This is almost identical to the bake she used to make us, but I brown my chicken legs before baking them as I think you get a better flavour that way. If you like you can skip this step and bung the dish straight in the oven. I also buy packets of pancetta cubes, as opposed to my mum's bacon, as I like the flavour, but again the choice is yours.

Serves 4

4-6 chicken legs, skin on
olive oil
knob of unsalted butter
100g cubed pancetta or
  streaky bacon
4 garlic cloves
250ml dry white wine
350g baby new potatoes,
  halved
250ml chicken stock
150g frozen peas
I tbsp roughly chopped mint
salt and pepper

Heat the oven to 200°C/gas 6. Rub the chicken legs with a little olive oil and season them with salt and pepper. Take a large ovenproof dish that you can also pop on the hob (a Le Creuset works well, but if you don't have one just brown the chicken in a frying pan then transfer it to a baking dish). Add 1 tablespoon of oil to the dish and place over a medium heat, then add the butter. When the butter has melted add the chicken legs, skin side down, and leave to brown, then flip the legs over and brown on the other side, spooning the butter over the meat. Add the pancetta and cook until browned all over.

Smash the garlic cloves and add to the dish, splash in the wine and give everything a good stir while it's bubbling away. Add the potatoes, stock and seasoning, then transfer to the oven and bake for 30 minutes. Add the peas and bake for a further 5-10 minutes, just to cook through. Rmove from the oven, toss through the mint and serve.

Dhruv's Mum's Easy Chicken Curry

Raised in India, my friend Dhruv was first taught to make this curry by his mum when he was 11. I love his food and am always begging him for a fantastic curry recipe so he finally shared this one with me. He says that if you have never made curry before, this one is a good starting point as it will teach you how to cook out spices and stop them from burning. He makes this for his boys and I now make it for Billie. She likes a little bit of kick, but this curry is not too spicy so it's great for most children. It's also a very versatile recipe, so once you've mastered this chicken version you could try cooking fish or vegetables instead.

Serves 4-6

2 tbsp vegetable oil
6 cloves
4 green cardamom pods
I cinnamon stick
2 onions, finely chopped
4cm piece of fresh root
    ginger, finely chopped
4 garlic cloves, crushed
I tsp turmeric powder
4 tsp ground coriander
2 tsp ground cumin
½ tsp chilli powder
250g tomatoes, blended
8 boneless, skinless
    chicken thighs, cut in
    half
250ml chicken stock
small bunch of coriander,
    chopped, to garnish
salt and pepper

Heat the oil in a lidded non-stick frying pan. When hot, add the cloves, cardamom and cinnamon and fry over a medium heat for about 3–4 minutes. Add the onions and fry for 10-15 minutes or until golden. Add the ginger and garlic and cook for a further 2 minutes. Add the turmeric, coriander, cumin and chilli and fry for 10 minutes; if it starts to stick add a tablespoon of water until it evaporates, then add another tablespoon and repeat.

Add the tomatoes and cook for 10 minutes, then add the chicken pieces and cook, covered, for 5 minutes. Pour in the stock and continue to cook, covered, for another 10 minutes. Uncover, turn up the heat and cook for another 10 minutes until the chicken is cooked through and the sauce has started to thicken. Season to taste and garnish with the fresh coriander.

Turkey Schnitzel and Chik Chak Salad

Emma was a 2015 *MasterChef* finalist, so of course we share a love of food. She also lives up the road from me and has become a really good friend; our girls go off and play together leaving us to discuss all things food to our hearts' content. As a fantastic cook, she's always feeding her children interesting things and when I asked her to give me a recipe to try with Billie, this is what she gave me. A 'chik chak' salad is an Israeli chopped vegetable salad. The recipe is taken from Emma's debut cookbook, *Fress*. I am not a huge lover of turkey but these schnitzels are incredible; I think it's soaking them in the egg, paprika and garlic that makes them so tender and super tasty. The schnitzels are now one of Billie's favourite things.

Serves 4

4 boneless turkey steaks
3 eggs
I tsp sweet paprika
2 garlic cloves, crushed
I75g panko breadcrumbs
sunflower oil
salt and pepper

For the chik chak salad

I cucumber
200g cherry tomatoes
I00g radishes
½ yellow pepper
I00g stuffed olives (I like
   the ones stuffed with
   pimento)
½ red onion, finely chopped

For the dressing

juice of I lemon (squeeze
   over ½ to begin with and
   add the rest if needed)
3 tbsp good-quality extra
   virgin olive oil
½ tsp sea salt
cracked black pepper
I tsp sumac

Lay a turkey steak between two sheets of cling film and use a rolling pin to lightly pound the meat until it's around 4-5mm thick. Repeat with the remaining steaks.

For the salad, split the cucumber in half lengthways, scoop out and discard the seeds, then chop the flesh into small cubes. Quarter the tomatoes, halve or quarter the radishes, then deseed and chop the pepper into small cubes. Put the chopped vegetables into a bowl with the olives and red onion. Add all the dressing ingredients, then add more oil and lemon juice if needed; you want it to be nice and sharp.

Whisk the eggs in a large shallow dish, wide enough to hold the turkey steaks in a single layer, then add the paprika and crushed garlic and season generously with salt and pepper. Lay the steaks in the mixture, turning to coat, cover with cling film and leave to marinate for at least two hours but preferably overnight.

Lay out the panko breadcrumbs on a large plate, then coat the egg-soaked turkey steaks in the breadcrumbs.

Fill a large, high-sided frying pan with oil to a depth of around 0.5cm and place over a medium heat. Test if the oil is hot enough by dropping in a breadcrumb; when it sizzles, it's ready. Fry the turkey steaks for around 4 minutes on each side until golden brown.Remove to a plate lined with kitchen towel to soak up any excess oil, then serve with the salad.

Clementine's Red Duck Curry

The power of social media continues to astound me and I love that friendships can be made from the other side of the world. I mentioned my 'Twitter friend' Clementine in my last book as I love her tweets and ended up asking her for the recipe for her orange almond cake, which is still one of my go-to cake recipes. Since I wrote *Tea and Cake*, I have had the pleasure of meeting Clementine (albeit briefly) in Melbourne and she gave me a jar of her favourite chilli jam, which she uses in this recipe.

This duck curry is delicious, but also surprisingly easy. Most supermarkets sell leg portions of duck and most stock chilli jam. Make sure you buy the jam and not the Thai chilli dipping sauce as that is too sweet and a different thing altogether! I like the duck meat because the texture stands up to a long braise, but you could substitute chicken legs and/or thighs if you'd prefer.

Serves 6-8

4 duck legs, skin on
I-2 tbsp Thai red curry
   paste
2 tbsp chilli jam
2 x 400g tins of coconut
   milk
2 tsp fish sauce
2 tsp soy sauce
I x 400g tin lychees in
   syrup, drained
I50ml sunflower oil
5 banana shallots, finely
   sliced
I bunch Thai basil
4 limes, to serve
basmati rice and roti,
   to serve

Heat a large frying pan over a medium heat. Add the duck legs, skin side down, and fry for 10 minutes until the skin is golden brown and the fat rendered. Put the duck legs into a heavy casserole dish that can also be used on the hob.

Put the curry paste and chilli jam into the frying pan and cook over a medium heat, until fragrant. Add the coconut milk and simmer for 10 minutes. Add the fish sauce and soy sauce to taste, then add the lychees and stir.

Heat the oven to 160°C/gas 3 (if using). Pour the curry sauce over the duck and either simmer it over a low heat on the hob or cook in the oven for around 2-3 hours, keeping an eye on it and checking the tenderness of the meat. Once it's coming off the bone easily, remove from the heat.

Towards the end of the cooking time, heat the sunflower oil in a frying pan over a low heat and gently fry the sliced shallots for 15-20 minutes, stirring occasionally, until golden brown all over. Scoop out with a slotted spoon and drain on kitchen towel.

Scatter the Thai basil and crispy shallots over the top of the duck legs and serve with the lime wedges and rice or roti on the side.

Cheat's Crispy Duck and Pancakes

I made this recipe up when I couldn't wait for a Chinese takeaway. The takeaway said it would take them at least an hour to deliver, which I suppose any sane person would just wait for, but I decided to set myself the challenge of making the same thing in that time instead. I ran to the shops, picked up duck breasts, pancakes and cucumber and hurried back to make my own version. It's not exactly the same, but I think it's pretty good, and if you've already bought your ingredients it's ready in under half an hour.

Serves 4

2 duck breasts, skin on
I tsp Chinese five spice
I tsp sea salt
½ cucumber
bunch of spring onions
8 Chinese pancakes
hoisin or plum sauce,
    to serve

Score the skin of the duck and rub with a little of the five spice and most of the salt. Place a non-stick frying pan over a high heat and lay the duck breasts in skin side down. Cook for 10 minutes until the skin is very crispy and the fat rendered out. Pour away most of the fat then sprinkle the meat side with the rest of the five spice and salt. Turn the breasts over and cook for 5 minutes before turning them back over on to the skin side to cook for a minute or two more. Set aside on a plate to rest.

Peel and deseed the cucumber and cut into thin matchsticks. Halve the spring onions and slice each one lengthways into thin matchsticks. Fill a bowl with cold water and ice and drop the spring onions into it.

Warm the pancakes according to the packet instructions. Finely slice the crispy-skinned duck breasts, and drain and pat dry the spring onions. Serve the pancakes with a splodge of hoisin or plum sauce, slices of the duck and a few cucumber and spring onion pieces.

SUSAN YOUNG

Chicken and Kale Bake

CANDY GILLIBRAND

Chicken Fiesta

JAY HUNT

Tarragon Chicken & Peppers

JULIET BAIRFELT

Chicken Soup

FERN BRITTON

Jubbly Pie

LEISL RAMPONO

Red Duck Curry

NINA PATERSON

Chicken Parcels

DHRUV BAKER

Easy Chicken Curry

NICOLA IBISON

Stuffed Roast Chicken

JOANIE BEESLEY

Red Chicken

EMMA SPITZER

Turkey Schnitzel

MEAT

✳ ✳ ✳ ✳ ✳ ✳

Summer Sausage and Sourdough Bake

Super Saucy Ribs with Corn Smash

Pork and Papaya Larb

Nicola's Lancashire Hotpot

Sausage and Apple Picnic Pie

Apple and Stilton One-pan Pork Chops

Easy Peasy Pizza

Dublin Coddle

Ham Hock Carbonara

Ann's Cheese Cracker Crumb Quiche

Oven-Baked Gammon with Celeriac Remoulade

Courgette and Dolcelatte Risotto
with Parma Ham Crisp

Butternut Squash Spaghetti with Lamb, Mint and Feta

Justine's Spanish Lamb Casserole

Lamb Chops and Skordalia

Cheat's Moussaka

Humble Roast

Koftas

Leftover Pot-luck Pies

Mrs E's Cottage Pie

Spanish Beef with Romesco Sauce

Mincey Beef 'Galette'

Vietnamese Beef Salad

Minute Steak and Rösti

Summer Sausage and Sourdough Bake

My niece Lola recently turned 18 and as well as having a 'no adults allowed' party, she also had a birthday lunch with all the family. Even though a lot of her family are vegetarian, there are a good number of meat eaters among the extended family too, so I offered to cook a meaty option for them. This is a one-tray wonder - easily transportable, and the bread goes all crispy and chewy and delicious in the stock. It went down a storm.

Serves 4

8 sausages
2 red onions, cut into
   wedges
I head of garlic, cloves
   separated and peeled
500g new potatoes, cut in
   half if large
200g sourdough bread,
   roughly torn into 2.5cm
   pieces
olive oil
I50ml chicken stock
handful of flat-leaf
   parsley, chopped
salt and pepper

Heat the oven to 200°C/gas 6.

Place the sausages, onion, garlic, potatoes and bread into a roasting tin and drizzle with a good amount of olive oil. Season well and roast for 15 minutes.

Give everything a stir to turn things over, pour over the chicken stock, then return the tray to the oven for a further 10-12 minutes until the sausages are browned, sticky and delicious. Scatter over the parsley before serving.

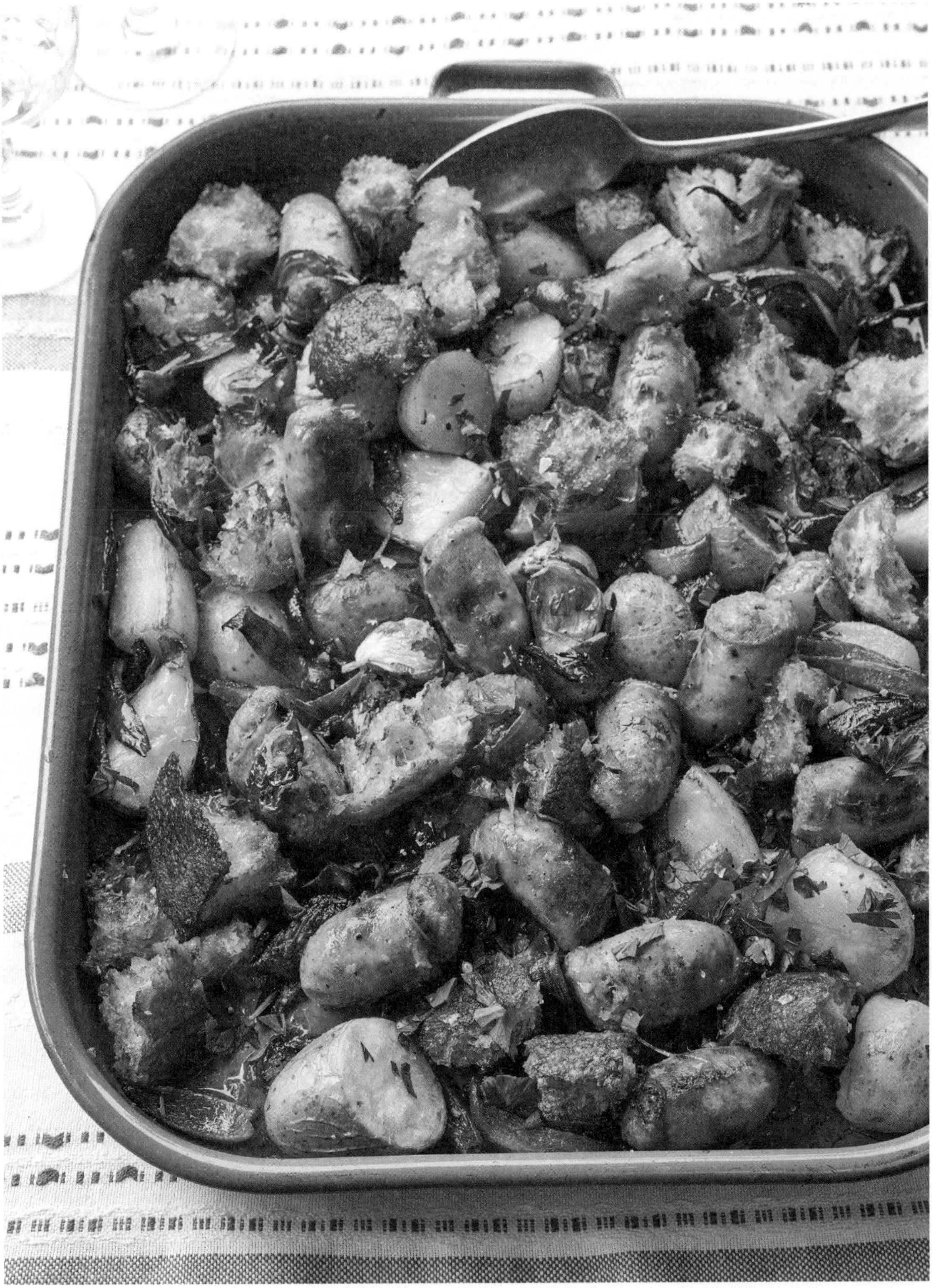

Super Saucy Ribs with Corn Smash

I have lost count of the number of times my friend Lauren has come to my rescue by taking Billie to school when I've been poorly or have been given a last-minute job. Having a strong network of local mum friends is a lifesaver! These ribs are Lauren's family's favourite supper. Children love ribs because it's the one time they're allowed to be messy. There are no knives and forks involved so they're just pure fun! The Tabasco gives these a little zing, and the vinegar and orange juice make the sauce lovely and tangy. Potato wedges or chips go very well with these, but I love the chunky smashed corn and potato which holds its texture but mops up the sauce perfectly.

Serves 6-8

180ml runny honey
150ml soy sauce
270ml tomato ketchup
good shake of Tabasco sauce
3 garlic cloves, bashed
3 heaped tsp English mustard
   powder
2 tsp hot smoked paprika
3 tsp sweet smoked paprika
450ml fresh orange juice
225ml red wine vinegar
2.5kg pork spare ribs

For the corn smash

1kg new potatoes
5 spring onions, roughly
   chopped
1 x 300g tin sweetcorn,
   drained and rinsed
2-3 tbsp olive oil
salt and pepper

To marinate the ribs, combine all the ingredients except the ribs. Place the ribs in a large, shallow dish, pour over the marinade and make sure all the ribs are coated. Leave to marinate for at least 3 hours or ideally overnight.

Heat the oven to 160°C/gas 3.

Lift the ribs into a large roasting tin and brush with a ladleful of the marinade, reserving any extra. Cover tightly with foil and roast for 2-3 hours until really tender and the meat is falling from the bones. At this point you can leave them to cool until you are ready to finish them off in the oven or on a hot barbecue.

Pour the leftover marinade into a pan along with any juices from the roasting tin. Bubble to reduce until thick and sticky then set aside.

Meanwhile, make the smash. Scrub the potatoes, place in a large pan of cold water and bring to the boil. Simmer for 20 minutes or until cooked. Drain and return to the pan with the spring onions, sweetcorn, olive oil and salt and pepper. Place over a low heat and use the back of a spoon to crush the potatoes, heat the corn and smash everything together. Reheat on a low heat when needed.

To finish the ribs, increase the oven setting to 200°C/gas 6 or heat a barbecue. Finish the ribs in the tin in the oven or directly on the barbecue, turning them every so often if on the barbecue, for 20-30 minutes, until dark, sticky and irresistible. Serve warm with the reheated corn smash.

Pork and Papaya Larb

Larb is a weird word and when I first heard it I wasn't at all sure what to expect. From Laos, it's best described as a dry spiced mince served wrapped in a lettuce leaf. I definitely think John's love of Asian food has rubbed off on me. Before I met him I wasn't very confident about cooking it and it was always something I would go out to eat. John has changed all that and I realise that with a little bit of encouragement and a few spices I'm actually pretty good. I love making this for a weekend lunch and washing it down with a cold beer. Make more than you need – the leftovers are really good in a tortilla wrap. And use lots of herbs – the more the bettter!

Note that this recipe calls for Thai basil, which has an amazing, unique flavour. It really is worth trying to track this down as lots of supermarkets stock it, If you can't find Thai basil you could use ordinary basil, but sadly it's not the same.

Serves 4

I tbsp groundnut oil
400g minced pork
I tsp chilli powder
I-2 tbsp fish sauce
4 tbsp cooked sticky or
    long grain rice (I use the
    pre-cooked rice)
I banana shallot, finely
    sliced
I red chilli, finely sliced
juice of 2 limes, plus extra
    to taste
salt

For the papaya salad

I green bird's eye chilli
I fat garlic clove
50g fine green beans
2 tbsp roasted peanuts
2 tsp dried shrimp paste
I tbsp palm sugar or soft
    light brown sugar
6 cherry tomatoes, quartered
juice of 2 limes
I tbsp fish sauce
I green, unripe papaya

For the larb, heat the oil in a wok, add the pork with a good splash of water and a pinch of salt and fry over a medium heat until the water has evaporated and the pork is cooked but not browned. Add the chilli powder and cook for about a minute then add the fish sauce and the rice and stir to combine.

Remove from the heat and leave to cool for 5 minutes. Tip the shallots, chilli and lime juice into the pork and mix well. Season with salt – the pork needs to be well seasoned.

Make the dressing for the salad: in a pestle and mortar or small food processor, pound the chilli, garlic, beans, peanuts, shrimp paste and sugar into a paste.

Tip into a bowl and add the tomatoes, lime juice and fish sauce.

continued overleaf ···>

large bunch each of
    mint, Thai basil and
    coriander, leaves picked,
    plus extra to garnish
2 Little Gem lettuces,
    leaves separated
chopped roasted peanuts

Peel the papaya then either shred it into fine strips in a food processor, or by cutting it into matchsticks with a sharp knife.

When ready to eat, stir big handfuls of the chopped herbs through the cooled larb: it should be hot, sour, bitter and salty; add extra lime juice if you like.

Spoon the larb into the lettuce leaves and serve with the papaya salad scattered with extra chopped peanuts and coriander, mint and Thai basil leaves.

Nicola's Lancashire Hotpot

My best friend Nicola always says she is not a good cook and then pulls brilliant things like this out of the bag. This is in fact an old recipe of her mum's that she learned when she was growing up, and she sent me lovely emails from her mum explaining what and how they used to cook and how much housekeeping money she had and what she would buy. In those days they would use whatever meat was on offer – often lamb or mutton, which is why she frequently turned to this traditional Lancashire stew, named after the pot in which it was typically made. The butcher would occasionally have braising steak at an economical price so Nicola's mum would sometimes use that and I really like it. This is a great pot of comfort food to warm the whole family on those dreary rainy days – I have simply added the ale to give it a richer flavour.

Serves 4-6

60g plain flour
600g braising steak, cut
  into chunks
2-3 tbsp vegetable oil
2 onions, sliced
3 carrots, chopped
2 celery sticks, chopped
300ml beef stock
200ml ale
good splash of
  Worcestershire sauce
4 thyme sprigs
I bay leaf
900g potatoes (Maris Piper
  work well), thinly sliced
40g unsalted butter, melted
salt and pepper

Heat the oven to 180°C/gas 4.

Put the flour into a freezer bag with a little salt and pepper, add the chunks of steak and give the bag a good shake until the meat is coated with the seasoned flour.

Heat the oil in a medium-sized casserole dish suitable for the hob and brown the steak in batches; don't overcrowd the pan or the meat won't brown. Once all the steak is browned, return it to the pan with the onions, carrots, celery, stock, ale, Worcestershire sauce and herbs and bring to the boil. Top with the potatoes, overlapping the slices, then cover and cook in the oven for 1½ hours.

Remove the dish from the oven and increase the oven temperature to 200°C/gas 6. Uncover the dish, brush the potatoes with the melted butter and cook for another 30 minutes until the potatoes are golden.

Sausage and Apple Picnic Pie

My make-up artist Justine, who has been making me up for most of my jobs for the past six years, has become a good friend, and her friend Philippa gave her this recipe. It's perfect for taking on family picnics or to parties when you are asked to bring a dish, as it's great served warm, cold or at room temperature and is a real winner with all the family.

Serves 6

500g pack all-butter
   shortcrust pastry
I tbsp light olive oil or
   vegetable oil
I onion, finely chopped
   2-3 thyme sprigs
I25g streaky bacon, finely
   chopped
I Granny Smith apple
400g sausage meat (or
   squeeze the filling from
   6 sausages)
2 tsp Dijon mustard
I egg, beaten
salt and pepper

Grease a 20cm loose-bottomed round sandwich tin.

Roll out the pastry slightly larger than the tin base and sides, then place it inside the tin and press into the corners and sides. Roll another disc to fit on the top and set aside.

In a pan, heat the oil and add the onion and thyme. Cook slowly over a low heat until soft, then add the chopped bacon and cook through; I like to get a bit of colour on the bacon. Set aside and, when cool, remove the thyme sprigs.

Peel and grate the apple and add to the bacon and onions along with the sausage meat, mustard and seasoning. Stir to combine thoroughly then press the mixture into the pastry case.

Brush the beaten egg around the rim and then press down the pastry lid, sealing the edges by pressing around the rim with a fork. Put two little holes in the top and cut out any pastry shapes you want to decorate with. Chill in the fridge for at least 20-30 minutes.

Heat the oven to 180°C/gas 4.

Egg wash the top of the pie and pastry shapes, and bake for 40-50 minutes until golden. Serve hot or cold.

Apple and Stilton One-pan Pork Chops

My friend Francine cooks with her friend Sarah every Friday, then they write up the recipes they like in their own recipe books, which they keep for their families. If they're all as good as this one then I would love to get my hands on those books and cook my way through them. I think it's wonderful that these two women get together every week and just cook and chat! In this recipe it's the cheese that was a real surprise and made the dish for me. Cooking blue cheese always helps soften its flavour and here it works so well with the sweetness of the apples. John, Billie and I had it for supper one night, and although I did leave the cheese off Billie's portion as she refused to try it (so you could do the same for your kids), John and I absolutely loved it. Have some crusty bread on hand – we couldn't stop mopping up the sauce.

Heat the oven to 200°C/gas 6.

Parboil the potatoes in a pan of boiling salted water for 10 minutes. Drain and set aside.

Heat the oil and butter in a large ovenproof frying pan. Season the chops, cut through the fat with a pair of scissors in a couple of places then brown over a high heat until golden. Set aside on a plate. Add the onion to the pan and cook for 10 minutes then remove and set aside.

Cut the apple into 8 wedges, discarding the core, then nestle the wedges in the frying pan with the potatoes. Add the onions then pour in the cider and stock. Season well and cook in the oven for 15 minutes until the potatoes are tender. Return the chops to the pan and cook in the oven for a further 10 minutes. Crumble over the cheese and return to the oven for 2-3 minutes until melted.

Melt the butter in a small pan and fry the sage leaves until crisp. Serve the pork and potatoes with the crispy fried sage leaves and crusty bread.

Serves 4

500g new potatoes, halved
    lengthways
1 tbsp olive oil
25g unsalted butter
4 chunky bone-in pork loin
    chops
1 onion, finely chopped
1 eating apple
100ml cider
100ml hot vegetable stock
75g Stilton cheese
salt and pepper
crusty bread, to serve

For the crispy sage leaves
25g unsalted butter
10 small sage leaves

Easy Peasy Pizza

I first created these quick pizzas for a programme I made about cooking with children. My own daughter and nephews and nieces love making these by themselves, and even when we go on holiday we buy the dough ingredients from the local supermarket so that they can whip up a quick pizza for lunch.

Serves 4

I x 400g tin chopped
  tomatoes
I tsp dried mixed herbs,
  plus extra for topping
2 pinches caster sugar
I garlic clove, grated
200g mozzarella (or use
  other cheeses you like -
  Cheddar or gorgonzola
  both work well), torn or
  crumbled into pieces
selection of toppings:
  ham, salami, peppers,
  sweetcorn, peas,
  courgettes, tuna, olives,
  spinach, etc.
salt and pepper

For the dough
300g self-raising flour,
  plus extra for dusting
I tsp baking powder
½ tsp salt
300g natural yoghurt

Heat the oven to 220°C/gas 7 and place 2 baking sheets in the oven to heat up.

To make the sauce, put the tomatoes, mixed herbs, sugar and garlic in a pan over a medium heat. Simmer gently for 10 minutes until thickened and of a spoonable consistency, then remove from the heat and season with salt and pepper. Leave to cool.

To make the dough, combine the flour, baking powder and salt in a bowl and make a well in the middle. Pour in the yoghurt then stir with a fork to combine. When the mixture forms a rough dough, turn out on to a lightly floured work surface and knead to form a smooth ball. Divide the dough into 4 equal pieces and roll out into thin circles.

Carefully remove the hot baking trays from the oven and lay the pizza bases on top, then bake for 3-4 minutes until beginning to rise. Remove from the oven.

Turn the pizza bases over and top with the sauce. Scatter the mozzarella over the top then add a selection of your favourite toppings. Season with pepper, sprinkle over a pinch of dried mixed herbs, then return to the oven and bake for 5 minutes until the cheese is golden and bubbling.

Dublin Coddle

This recipe was passed down to my friend Amanda Byram by her Irish grandmother, who always had a pot bubbling away on her stove. It's a stew made by Dubliners, not dissimilar to a classic Irish stew, but using bacon and sausages instead of the traditional Irish lamb. Her choice of recipe slightly surprised me, as Amanda is a firm member of the healthy eating gang! With its hefty dose of potatoes and pearl barley to bulk it, this is proper comfort food. The carnivore in me loves the meatiness, and as I've said, I'm a big fan of one-pot meals. Serve this one with seasonal veg and a glass of Guinness.

Serves 4-6

sunflower oil
8 sausages (any type you like)
250g streaky bacon
2 onions, finely sliced
100g pearl barley
2 carrots, sliced
handful of flat-leaf parsley, chopped
750g potatoes, thickly sliced
700ml beef or chicken stock
salt and pepper

Heat the oven to 150°C/gas 2.

Heat a little oil in a frying pan and brown the sausages all over. Remove the sausages from the pan then fry the bacon until starting to colour. Cut the sausages and bacon into bite-sized pieces and set aside.

Add a little more oil to the pan and gently fry the onions for 5 minutes until softened. Tip into a bowl with the pearl barley, carrots and parsley. Season well with salt and pepper and mix together.

Place half the sausages and bacon into a lidded casserole dish suitable for the hob, top with half the veggies and pearl barley, then a layer of potatoes on top. Repeat the layering once more, finishing with a final layer of potato, then pour over the stock. Bring to the boil, then cover and transfer to the oven for 2½-3 hours until you have a rich, thick sauce. Check the pot after 2 hours and add a little more stock if necessary.

Ham Hock Carbonara

I remember Billie coming back from her first overnight school trip. I picked her up, covered in mud and smiles, in desperate need of a cuddle (me), a bath (her) and a big steaming bowl of comfort food (us both). Almost every cook has their favourite way to make carbonara and this is mine. Using ham hock instead of bacon just provides a quick fix and saves you some time as it's already cooked, but I also really like the texture.

Serves 4

200g baby broad beans or
    frozen broad beans
350g spaghetti or other
    long pasta
2 medium eggs, beaten
200g shredded ham hock
finely grated zest of
    I lemon
2-3 tbsp double cream
35g Parmesan, grated
handful of flat-leaf
    parsley, finely chopped
salt and pepper

Cook the broad beans in a pan of boiling water for 2 minutes. Drain and cool under cold running water, then slip the bright green beans out of their outer skins and set aside.

Cook the pasta in boiling salted water for 10-12 minutes until just cooked. Drain, then return the pasta to the pan, add the beaten egg and stir over a low heat to cook the egg. Add the rest of the ingredients and mix together, season with plenty of pepper and serve immediately.

Ann's Cheese Cracker Crumb Quiche

Using cheese crackers as a base for a quiche may sound surprising but they're a really great substitute for pastry. It isn't nearly as much faff as making pastry from scratch, and although the end result is more spongy than crisp, it works with the filling. This is my godmother Ann's recipe, and it is quite rich but the first time I made it I couldn't stop going back for another slice!

Serves 6-8

For the base
175g Ritz Crackers
80g unsalted butter, melted
70g grated Gruyère cheese

For the filling
200g cherry tomatoes
olive oil
8 rashers streaky bacon,
  finely chopped
1 onion, finely sliced
2 eggs
150ml single cream
50g grated Gruyère cheese
salt and pepper

Heat the oven to 200°C/gas 6.

Whiz the crackers in a food processor until they form crumbs, then whiz in the melted butter and Gruyère. Press into the base and sides of a 22cm loose-bottomed fluted tart tin. Bake in the oven for about 10 minutes until dark golden, then remove from the oven and set aside.

For the filling, place the tomatoes on a baking tray, drizzle with a little olive oil and cook for about 30 minutes until soft but still holding their shape. Reduce the oven temperature to 180°C/gas 4.

While the tomatoes are cooking, heat a little oil in a frying pan and fry the bacon until crisp. Remove from the pan with a slotted spoon and transfer to a bowl. Add the onion to the pan and fry gently for 10 minutes until softened and golden. Add to the bowl with the bacon.

In a bowl, beat the eggs, cream and Gruyère together, season with salt and pepper and stir in the bacon and onion. Pour into the tart tin then dot all over with the roasted tomatoes, pushing them into the mixture a little. Place on a baking tray and bake for 20-25 minutes until just set. Remove from the tin and serve.

Oven-Baked Gammon with Celeriac Remoulade

Viv is my friend Meredith's mum; she is a force of nature and I love hearing Merry's stories. I think of the remoulade as a 70s dish that has been revived in recent years, and I think it's great served with the smoked gammon and a good old jacket spud!

Serves 4

5 carrots, unpeeled
Ikg smoked gammon joint

For the celeriac remoulade
2 tbsp Dijon mustard
2 tbsp vegetable oil
½ tbsp walnut oil
½ tbsp caster sugar
I tbsp white wine vinegar
I20ml single cream
I small celeriac
handful of flat-leaf
   parsley, chopped

Heat the oven to 180°C/gas 4.

Place the carrots whole in a roasting tin, lay the gammon on top and then pour in 250ml water. Cover the tin with baking parchment and tin foil and bake for 1 hour, then remove from the oven and leave to rest, covered, for 30 minutes.

For the celeriac remoulade, whisk together the mustard, oils, sugar and vinegar in a bowl until combined and the mixture goes from glossy to matte. Then stir in the cream gently as you don't want your sauce to thicken too much and split.

Peel and halve the celeriac, then, using a mandoline or grater, julienne the celeriac and stir it through the cream mixture with a good handful of chopped parsley.

Serve slices of the lovely warm (room temperature) gammon with the remoulade.

Courgette and Dolcelatte Risotto with Parma Ham Crisp

When I want an instant summer pick-me-up I make this risotto as it reminds me of holidays in the sunshine. Last year my family was lucky enough to spend a beautiful month in the south of France and this was a regular lunch, made with courgettes from our garden and some local soft blue cheese. With a glass of crisp white wine and the sun on my back, I was in heaven. The Parma ham crisp was a late addition – it adds a nice bit of texture and crunch.

Serves 4

I tbsp olive oil
good knob of unsalted
    butter
I banana shallot, finely
    sliced
350g Arborio rice
200ml dry white wine
750-850ml hot chicken stock
8 slices Parma ham
2 courgettes, grated
large handful of baby
    spinach
40g grated Parmesan
60g dolcelatte
salt and pepper

Heat the oven to 200°C/gas 6.

Heat the oil and butter in a frying pan. Add the shallots and fry gently over a low heat for 5 minutes until softened. Add the rice and cook in the buttery-ness for a minute or so until the rice becomes translucent. Pour in the wine, increase the heat to medium and cook, stirring, until it has all been absorbed.

Season well then add a good ladleful of stock and cook, stirring, until it is absorbed before adding the next ladleful. Continue to add more stock as each ladleful is absorbed.

Place the Parma ham between two baking sheets and roast in the oven for 10 minutes until it is lovely and crisp.

When there is only one ladleful of stock remaining, add the courgette and spinach and stir through. Remove from the heat, add the final ladleful of stock and the cheeses. Stir, then cover and leave to stand for 5 minutes. Serve with the Parma ham crisps.

Butternut Squash Spaghetti with Lamb, Mint and Feta

My cousin Harriet is a mother of two and lives in New York. She says she gets very homesick, so when I asked her for a recipe idea she said that she cooks from my first book all the time because it reminds her of our childhood and of home. She loves making our family Bolognese sauce but is always trying to find different ways to serve it. In America, spaghetti squash is widely available when in season and, once cooked, almost resembles spaghetti. In the UK it's harder to find so I have adapted her original recipe and have use 'spiralised' squash noodles. If you have a spiraliser, it takes minutes to make these yourself, or the noodles are now available to buy in some supermarkets. Failing that, roasting a squash, scooping out the centre and serving the lamb inside is also wonderful. The lamb 'Bolognese' is truly delicious and a great take on a good old classic.

Serves 4

olive oil
I large onion, sliced
I large garlic clove,
    crushed
400g minced lamb
200ml dry white wine
I x 400g tin chopped
    tomatoes
I tbsp tomato purée
400ml chicken stock
good grating of nutmeg
I large butternut squash
I tbsp chopped mint, plus
    a few extra leaves for
    garnish
150g feta cheese
salt and pepper

Heat 1 tablespoon of oil in a sauté pan and gently fry the onion for 10 minutes until really soft and golden. Add the garlic and fry for another minute, then add the lamb. Increase the heat and fry, breaking up the mince with a spatula, until it is browned all over.

Add the wine and bubble until reduced by half, then add the tomatoes, tomato purée and stock. Season well and simmer gently for 1½ hours, adding more stock if it gets a little too dry.

Meanwhile, heat the oven to 190°C/gas 5.

Peel the squash and use a spiraliser to spiralise the long part (body) into noodles. Cut the bulb in half and scoop out the seeds. Put the 'bowls' in a roasting tin, season and drizzle with oil, then roast for 30-40 minutes, adding the noodles after about 20 minutes with another drizzle of oil. Roast until the noodles and bowls are tender.

Stir the mint into the 'Bolognese' sauce. Serve the roasted noodles with the sauce and scatter over the feta cheese and mint leaves. Save the roasted bowls for another time or you could serve these as well.

Justine's Spanish Lamb Casserole

Growing up we would often go on holiday to Spain so I have been really influenced by Spanish flavours - garlic, paprika and parsley are my idea of heaven. Spanish food is also a very family-friendly cuisine; kids feel like they're eating something quite grown up and exotic, but the spice in chorizo is actually very mild and suits their palates. My make-up artist Justine's husband Danny is Spanish, so I was hopeful that if I asked her for a recipe I was likely to get something I'd love. This is Danny's father's recipe. Justine's two boys devour this dish and it has now become a firm favourite in my house too. Don't be put off by the lamb neck - it's a great braising meat and whereas some people find lamb quite a strong flavour, the meat from the neck is actually much milder. It's also a very economical cut.

Serves 4

olive oil
3-4 lamb neck fillets (about
    600g), cut into 2cm
    pieces
400g cooking chorizo,
    chopped
100ml dry sherry
2 onions, chopped
2 green peppers, chopped
2 garlic cloves, crushed
2 tsp sweet smoked paprika
½ x 400g tin chopped
    tomatoes or 6 fresh
    tomatoes, chopped
6 medium waxy potatoes,
    cut into thirds
1 litre chicken stock
3 bay leaves
1 x 400g tin chickpeas,
    drained and rinsed
150g spinach
salt and pepper
crusty bread, to serve

Heat 2 tablespoons of oil in a pan. Season the lamb, then add to the pan and brown, in batches if necessary, until golden all over. Remove and set aside.

Add another 2 tablespoons of oil to the pan and fry the chorizo for 5 minutes until golden and its oils are released. Scoop out with a slotted spoon then deglaze the pan by splashing in the sherry and letting it bubble away until almost completely evaporated. Add a little more oil then gently fry the onions and peppers for 10 minutes until softened. Add the garlic and paprika and cook for 30 seconds then add the tomatoes.

Return the lamb and chorizo to the pan. Add the potatoes then pour over the stock and add the bay leaves. Season and bring to the boil then reduce the heat and simmer gently for 1 hour until the lamb is very tender and the sauce thickened.

Add the chickpeas and spinach and allow the spinach to wilt before serving with crusty bread.

Lamb Chops and Skordalia

A few years ago, John and and I discovered Mykonos. We went just before the main summer season started, when the heat was still bearable and the sea crisp and calm. We stayed at a beautiful, very small hotel, swam every morning and then we would chat to the charming waiter about what to do and where to go to eat. One of the restaurants we discovered there was a fish restaurant called Markos. At times we were the only people there and we fell in love with the place – I took so many pictures of the fresh fish and the kitchens! One day John and I shared a huge lunch of fresh fish, salad, beetroot, crispy lamb chops and, my favourite thing – *skordalia* – a puréed potato and garlic dish. We drank cold beer and Greek wine and chatted and ate in the sunshine. The *skordalia* I've re-created here isn't *too* garlicky, but if you're going to make it for a hot date, make sure that both of you eat it.

Serves 4

8–12 lamb cutlets or chops
(about 3 cutlets or 2 chops
per person)
60ml olive oil
juice of 1 lemon
handful of oregano, chopped
handful of flat-leaf,
chopped parsley
salt and white pepper

For the skordalia
500g floury potatoes,
chopped
250ml olive oil
200ml milk
5 garlic cloves, peeled and
left whole
juice of 1 lemon

Place the chops in a large wide bowl. Combine the olive oil, lemon juice, herbs and seasoning, pour over the chops and leave to marinate for 1 hour in the fridge.

For the skordalia, put the potatoes into a heavy-based pan with 200ml of the olive oil, the milk and some salt and pepper, and place over a medium heat. Bring to the boil and cook for 15–20 minutes or until the potatoes are soft.

Meanwhile, place the remaining olive oil and the garlic in a small frying pan and cook slowly over a medium-low heat for about 10 minutes until the garlic is soft. Strain and set aside.

Remove the potatoes from the heat and strain the cooking liquid into a jug. Pass the potatoes through a masher or ricer and use a spatula to mix in the lemon juice and softened garlic. Gradually add some of the cooking liquid until smooth and creamy. Return this to the potato pan and reheat over a gentle heat while you cook the lamb. Use more of the reserved cooking liquid if it is too dry.

Heat your grill, griddle pan or barbecue until hot, then grill the lamb for approx 4–5 minutes on each side, depending on the size of your chops. Make sure the fat is nice and crispy and baste with any leftover marinade.

Serve the lamb chops with the skordalia and a lovely big green salad.

Cheat's Moussaka

Making a béchamel sauce alongside all the other bits you need for a traditional moussaka can be a bit of a faff, so I created this really easy cheat's version. The yoghurt sauce has a great tangy flavour, is much quicker to make and I can honestly say I prefer it to the classic white sauce.

Serves 4-6 depending on how hungry you are

4 large aubergines, sliced into Icm rounds
olive oil
I onion, chopped
2 garlic cloves, grated
I tsp ground cinnamon
I tsp ground cumin
500g minced lamb (you could also use beef)
2 x 400g tins chopped tomatoes
I tbsp tomato purée
splash of Worcestershire sauce
300g Greek yoghurt
IOOg Cheddar cheese, grated
I tbsp Dijon mustard
I egg
salt and pepper

Heat the oven to 180°C/gas 4.

Rub the aubergine rounds in a little olive oil, salt and pepper and place in the oven for about 20 minutes, until they have a little colour on them. Remove and set aside.

Heat a little olive oil in a large frying pan, add the onions and soften on a low heat for 5-10 minutes. Add the garlic and cook for a few minutes, just to soften it slightly, before adding the cinnamon, cumin and a splash of water. Cook the spices for 2-3 minutes then increase the heat to medium, add the mince and brown it all over. Pour in the tomatoes, tomato purée and Worcestershire sauce, season, then bring to the boil and simmer for about 30 minutes, until the lamb is cooked through.

In a bowl, mix together the yoghurt, Cheddar, mustard and egg.

Place a layer of the aubergine rounds in the base of an ovenproof dish, about 25 x 25cm (or a similar size), followed by a layer of mince, and repeat until both are used up. Pour over the yoghurt mixture and bake in the oven for about 30-40 minutes until golden and puffed up.

Humble Roast

My sister's friend Victoria is mother to three hungry boys, and a fantastic cook to boot! Victoria is a huge *MasterChef* fan and her family and friends are treated to some of the most amazing meals, including this delicious roast lamb. Being Jewish, the Friday night family roast is a tradition handed down through the generations. She likes to roast a large leg so there's plenty left over to fill wraps with salad and hummus for Saturday lunch! And once you've tasted these crunchy semolina roast potatoes, I guarantee you won't want to make anything else - they are that good! I've served this to my family with a simple salad made by shaving courgette into ribbons and tossing with a light olive oil and lemon dressing, but any seasonal salad or just some young leaves would be perfect - it just needs a little freshness.

Serves 6

2 red onions, cut into thin
  wedges
1 garlic bulb, cloves
  separated
2 fennel bulbs, finely
  sliced
3 tbsp olive oil
2 tsp sumac
2 tsp cumin seeds
1 tsp coriander seeds
2 tsp fennel seeds
2kg shoulder of lamb,
  bone in
125ml white wine
100ml chicken stock
salt and pepper

For the crunchy semolina roast potatoes

1.4kg King Edward or Maris
  Piper potatoes, cut into
  chunks
5 tbsp olive oil
3 tbsp semolina
5 garlic cloves, smashed

Heat the oven to 200°C/gas 6.

Put the onions, garlic and fennel into a large roasting tin. Toss with 2 tablespoons of the oil and season well.

Mix all the spices together. Drizzle the lamb with the last tablespoon of oil then rub the spices all over the shoulder, making sure they're evenly spread. Season well.

Place the lamb on top of the vegetables, then pour the wine and stock into the tin around it (not over it). Cook for 20 minutes, then cover the lamb with foil and reduce the oven temperature to 160°C/gas 3.

Roast the lamb for 2-2½ hours, until the meat is falling from the bone. Meanwhile, prepare the potatoes.

Put the potatoes into a pan of water, bring to the boil and simmer for 5 minutes. Drain and then return them to the dry pan. Coat with 1-2 tablespoons of olive oil and sprinkle with salt and pepper and the semolina. Shake the pan around to coat the potatoes.

continued overleaf ···>

About an hour or so before the end of the lamb's cooking time, put the remaining potato oil in a roasting tin in the oven until hot, then add the potatoes and garlic and stir to mix. Roast for about 45 minutes, until golden.

To finish the lamb and potatoes, lift the foil off the lamb and increase the heat to 200ºC/gas 6. Leave for 15 minutes or so to really brown the top of the meat and to crisp up the potatoes.

Serve the lamb with the semolina roasties and a seasonal salad.

Koftas

My friend Nadia is a very good cook, and these koftas – similar to meatballs – are her children's favourite dinner. Nadia serves them with potato wedges and salad but personally I love them in these home-made pitta breads with hummus or a spoonful of yoghurt. Once you have made these you will never want shop-bought pittas again! They both freeze really well too.

Serves 4

500g minced pork
small bunch of mint, finely
  chopped
small bunch of flat-leaf
  parsley, finely chopped
I onion, grated
3 tbsp Greek yoghurt, plus
  extra to serve
sunflower oil
300g cherry tomatoes,
  halved
2 tbsp extra virgin olive
  oil
handful of rocket or other
  leaves
salt and pepper

For the pitta breads
290ml water
7g sachet fast-action yeast
I tsp caster sugar
40ml vegetable oil
450g plain flour, plus
  extra for dusting
I tsp salt

Start by making the pitta breads as they need time to prove. Pour approximately 50ml of the water into a small jug or cup. Add the yeast and sugar and mix until combined. In a separate jug, mix the remaining water and the oil, then add the yeast and stir to combine.

Place the flour and salt into the bowl of a stand mixer. Using the dough hook, start mixing on a low speed, adding the yeast, water and oil mix. When combined, turn the speed to medium and mix for about 5 minutes until smooth and elastic.

Tip the dough into an oiled bowl and cover with oiled cling film for 1 hour; you don't want to leave the dough longer than this as you still want the yeast to be active when you cook the bread.

Meanwhile, put the minced pork, mint, parsley, onion, yoghurt and plenty of seasoning in a bowl and mix together. Shape into 24 small meatballs then chill in the fridge for at least 1 hour.

Heat the oven to 220°C/gas 7 and place two baking trays in the oven to heat up.

Transfer the dough to a lightly floured surface and knead a little flour in so that the dough is workable. Cut it into 8 balls and keep them under oiled cling film while you're working. Take a ball and roll it out flat – about 8-10cm long – using only a few strokes of the rolling pin, then repeat with the remaining balls.

continued overleaf •••>

Carefully remove the hot baking trays from the oven and lay 4 of the breads on top, 2 per tray, and cook for 3 minutes until you see the breads bubble up. Turn them over and cook for a further 3 minutes until golden and puffed up. Repeat with the remaining breads, keeping the cooked breads warm under a clean tea towel.

Heat a thin film of sunflower oil in a non-stick frying pan and fry the koftas for 5-6 minutes, turning regularly, until golden brown and cooked through.

Mix the tomatoes with the extra virgin olive oil and plenty of seasoning. Serve the koftas with the tomatoes in warm pitta breads with a handful of leaves.

Leftover Pot-luck Pies

Like me, my friend Kate always has leftovers from a roast and I think this is a great way of using them up. Any leftover meat or veg you have can go into these little pots, which are then topped with filo pastry. I love the crunch of filo pastry and it's a nice contrast to the soft cooked veg.

Serves 4

2 red or white onions, cut
    into wedges
3 carrots, cut into chunks
300g new potatoes, halved
    or quartered
handful of fresh thyme
    leaves or rosemary
2 tbsp olive oil
500g leftover roast lamb (or
    any other meat you might
    have had on a Sunday), or
    use cooked sausages
½ Savoy cabbage, finely
    sliced, or you could use
    peas, kale, broccoli or
    any other greens you like
450ml lamb or chicken stock
4 sheets filo pastry
50g melted unsalted butter
salt and pepper

Heat the oven to 200°C/gas 6.

Put the onion, carrot, potato and herbs into a roasting tin. Season and drizzle with oil then roast for 30 minutes, turning occasionally, until golden and just cooked. If you have any leftover roasted veg and potatoes from your Sunday roast you can use these instead of roasting more, or if you just have a few, add them to your roasting tin.

Cut the leftover lamb into chunks and combine with the roasted veg, cabbage and stock.

Divide between four 300ml pots. Brush the sheets of filo pastry with the melted butter and scrunch on top of the pies.

Place the pots on a baking tray and bake for 20-25 minutes until the pastry is golden and crisp. Serve immediately.

Mrs E's Cottage Pie

Frances is one of my walking buddies. I am always interested in how other people make 'the classics', so after a walk during which Frances and I had a good natter about cottage pie, I bought all the ingredients on the way home and cooked it that night for dinner. Since then I have slightly adapted the recipe and added boiled potatoes to the top because Billie doesn't like mash (I know – how?!) and also because the potatoes go nice and crispy.

Serves 4-6

I tbsp olive oil, plus extra
  to drizzle
I large onion, finely sliced
2 garlic cloves, crushed
500g minced beef
I x 400g tin chopped
tomatoes
I tbsp tomato purée
I x 400g tin cream of
  tomato soup (I use Heinz)
200g frozen peas or petit
  pois, defrosted
about I.4kg floury potatoes
salt and pepper

Heat the oil in a pan and fry the onions gently over a low heat for 10 minutes. Add the garlic and the beef and fry, breaking the mince up with a spoon, until the meat is browned all over. Add the tomatoes, tomato purée and soup. Season well then simmer for 1 hour until rich and delicious. Add a splash of water if it gets too thick at any point. Stir through the peas.

Heat the oven to 180°C/gas 4.

For the potatoes, fill a 30 x 23cm baking dish with as many potatoes as it fits (to work out how many you will need), then peel and place them in a pan of boiling water and boil them for around 20 minutes until tender. Drain and leave to cool. Break them up a little, season and drizzle with oil.

Spoon the mince into the baking dish, spoon the potatoes over the top, drizzle with a little more oil and bake in the oven for about 30 minutes until golden and bubbling.

Spanish Beef with Romesco Sauce

This is a great dish for when friends are coming round to dinner – you can marinate the meat and prepare the potatoes in advance, meaning you can just sit back and enjoy a lovely glass of Rioja with your mates, dreaming of Spain. The sauce also keeps for up to a week stored in an airtight container in the fridge – it's delicious as a dip.

Serves 4

1 beef rib (about 1–1.2kg)
handful of thyme leaves
2 tsp each hot smoked paprika and smoked sweet paprika
2 tbsp olive oil
4 large baking potatoes
4 spring onions, finely sliced
100g manchego cheese, grated
100g rocket leaves
salt and pepper

For the romesco sauce

1 x 200g tin chopped tomatoes
2 roasted red peppers from a jar, plus a little of the oil
1 garlic clove
100g ground almonds
1 tbsp white wine vinegar
1–2 tbsp olive oil
1 heaped tsp paprika

Heat the oven to 200°C/gas 6.

Put the beef in a dish with the thyme, paprika and oil. Season well and rub the marinade all over the meat. Set aside for 30 minutes to 1 hour.

Place the potatoes on a baking tray in the oven for 1 hour until really tender and the skins are crispy.

Meanwhile, put all the ingredients for the romesco sauce in a food processor and blitz together. Season with salt and pepper and set aside.

When the potatoes are cooked, remove from the oven and, when cool enough to handle, halve and scoop out the insides into a bowl, reserving the skins. Mix the potato with the spring onions and a good 2–3 tablespoons of the romesco sauce.

Heat an ovenproof heavy-based pan over a high heat and brown the beef rib all over. Transfer to the oven and roast for 20-25 minutes until cooked but still pink in the middle. Remove from the oven and allow to rest for at least 10 minutes.

Spoon the potato mixture back into the potato skins, place on a baking tray and scatter with the cheese. Return to the oven for 5-10 minutes until hot and melted.

Slice the beef and serve with the romesco potatoes, the rocket leaves and the rest of the sauce on the side.

Mincey Beef 'Galette'

Holidays are happy times for children (and adults, of course!) and food is often a big part of our memories: lunches in the sun, by a pool or at the beach are treasured moments. When I asked my friend Amanda what her children liked to eat, she didn't hesitate: her family makes these 'galettes' on their summer holidays in France. A French galette is actually made with a pastry base, but for simplicity Amanda and her children use tortillas as there's less mess and less fuss. A cross between a pizza, a quiche and a Bolognese sauce – what's not to love?!

Serves 4

olive oil
250g minced beef
I onion, finely chopped
2 garlic cloves, crushed
200g mushrooms, finely
   sliced
2 yellow peppers, finely
   sliced
2 tsp paprika
4 wholemeal tortilla wraps
200g Cheddar cheese, grated
4 eggs

Heat ½ a tablespoon of oil in a pan and fry the mince until it is browned all over. Remove from the pan and set aside. Add another ½ tablespoon of oil to the pan and fry the onions gently for 10 minutes. Add the garlic and mushrooms and fry over a high heat until the mushrooms are golden brown. Return the mince to the pan, add the peppers and paprika and cook for a further 10 minutes, with a splash of water, until everything is lovely and soft.

Place one of the tortillas in a frying pan over a medium heat, spoon a quarter of the mince mixture on to the tortilla and scatter with a quarter of the cheese. Cook until the cheese starts to melt.

Meanwhile, fry an egg in a little oil in a non-stick pan then serve the galette with the fried egg. Repeat with the rest of the tortillas, mince and eggs.

Vietnamese Beef Salad

This salad is my friend Vicks's go-to lunch dish. She is a fabulous cook and a really lovely friend, and hosts some of the most fun lunch and dinner parties I've ever been to. What's funny is that she (along with a lot of the mums in this book) doesn't think she's a very good cook, but something made with love for another person is always going to taste good! The first time I made this salad I couldn't stop eating it. I made double and ate it the next day, and then proceeded to make it every day for the rest of the week, it was that good... You really can't get enough of it!

Serves at least 6

3 large carrots, peeled into
   ribbons
½ cucumber, peeled
   lengthways into ribbons
   until you get to the seeds
2 tbsp rice wine vinegar
I tsp caster sugar
2 sirloin steaks
I tbsp olive oil
½ Chinese cabbage
good handful of beansprouts
I large bunch of Thai basil
large handful of mint
large handful of coriander
2 red chillies, finely sliced
salt and pepper

For the dressing
½ red onion, thinly sliced
I garlic clove, crushed
juice of 2 limes
I-2 tbsp fish sauce
2 tbsp rice wine vinegar
I tbsp caster sugar

Put the carrots and cucumber in a bowl with the vinegar and sugar and set aside to marinate for 30 minutes or so.

Mix all the ingredients for the dressing together in a bowl then set aside.

Rub the steaks with the oil and season well. Heat a pan or griddle over a high heat and fry the steaks for 1-2 minutes on each side, depending on thickness, until cooked but still rare in the middle. Set aside to rest on a plate.

Shred the cabbage into a bowl. Drain the carrot and cucumber and add to the cabbage with the beansprouts, herbs and chillies. Pour over the dressing and toss to combine.

Thinly slice the steaks, toss briefly with the salad and serve.

Minute Steak and Rösti

'Minute steak' is the general name for any thin piece of beef that can be cooked quickly, rather than describing which part of the animal it comes from as most cuts do. My mum was a big fan of minute steaks and we ate them a lot growing up, usually accompanied by a scooped out jacket potato (yum!). I like to serve mine with crispy rösti because you can prepare them in advance and then pop them in the oven about an hour before you know you want to eat. It means you've only got the steaks to worry about at the last minute!

Serves 4

Ikg floury potatoes
I onion
70g unsalted butter, melted
I tbsp plain flour
4 minute steaks
olive oil
salt and pepper
watercress, to garnish

Heat the oven to 200°C/gas 6. Line a 20cm square tin or a baking tray with baking parchment.

Grate the potatoes and the onion into a large heatproof dish (I try and squeeze out as much water as possible from the grated potato with my hands). Cover with boiling water and leave to sit for 2–3 minutes.

Drain, then place the potatoes and onion in a tea towel and squeeze out as much water as you can. Transfer to a bowl and add the melted butter, flour and lots of salt and pepper.

Press the potato mix into the tin or baking tray, cover loosely with foil and bake for 30 minutes. Increase the oven temperature to 220°C/gas 7, remove the foil and cook for a further 25 minutes until crispy and golden.

Oil the steaks and season well. Heat a frying pan, add a little oil to the pan and when it is really hot add the steaks. Flash fry for around 30 seconds on each side. Serve with the rösti and garnish with watercress.

AMANDA BYRAM

Dublin Coddle

LAUREN SHERMAN

Saucy Ribs

FRANCINE CORBIN

Apple and Stilton
Pork Chops

NADIA MARCOULLIDES

Koftas

PHILIPPA NORTCLIFFE

Sausage and
Apple Picnic Pie

VIVIEN PHILLIPS

Oven-Baked Gammon with
Celeriac Remoulade

ANN PHILLIPS

Cheese Cracker
Crumb Quiche

KATE MAGOWAN

Leftover Pot-Luck Pies

HARRIET INGHAM

**Butternut Squash Spaghetti
with Lamb, Mint & Feta**

VICTORIA DANGOOR

Humble Roast

JUSTINE GONZALEZ

Spanish Lamb Casserole

AMANDA FROST

Mincey Beef 'Galette'

FRANCES HARVEY

Mrs E's Cottage Pie

NICOLA STEPHENSON

Lancashire Hotpot

VICTORIA PALIN

Vietnamese Beef Salad

FISH

******

Coconut and Coriander Crusted Fish Bake
with Sweet Potato Wedges
Smoked Salmon Mousse on Rye with Pickled Cucumber
and Radish Salad
Prawn and Seafood Stick Salad
Spiced Crab Linguine
Spicy Sunshine Prawns with Feta Flatbreads
Fish Tacos
Baked Cod with Chorizo, Chickpeas
and Paprika Garlic Sauce
Lentils and Salmon
Sunita's Seafood Stew
Fish Fritters with Green Salsa
Salmon Teriyaki

Coconut and Coriander Crusted Fish Bake with Sweet Potato Wedges

When I was younger I wasn't keen on fish. I liked prawns and crab but a plain piece of fish never really did it for me. Now I can't get enough of it. I love very simply grilled fish with a little butter and lemon and a few fresh herbs, but I also love how versatile fish can be and how much flavour it can take on without being overpowered. Coriander and lemongrass really ramp up a humble cod or monkfish fillet, but the paste is also good on prawns or on top of a big juicy scallop. The world is your oyster!

Heat the oven to 200°C/gas 6.

Serves 4

4 x 175g chunky white fish
   fillets
groundnut oil

For the spice paste
large bunch of coriander,
   with stalks if you can
   get it
grated zest of 1 lime, plus
   a squeeze of lime juice
2 lemongrass sticks, finely
   chopped
100g fresh white
   breadcrumbs
3 tbsp coconut oil
2 tbsp unsweetened
   desiccated coconut
salt and pepper

For the sweet potato wedges
3 sweet potatoes
4 tbsp olive oil
1/2 tsp paprika

For the wedges, cut the potatoes in half lengthways and then in half lengthways again, and if they are still too chunky for you cut them again (I like thin, crispy ones). In a bowl, toss the wedges with the oil, paprika and some salt and pepper. Transfer to a large baking tray or roasting tin and roast in the oven for 25-30 minutes or until crispy. Remove from the oven, cover with foil to keep warm and lower the oven temperature to 180°C/gas 4.

Meanwhile, put all the ingredients for the spice paste into a small food processor and whizz to form a paste. Season well with salt and pepper.

Place the fish in a small roasting tin and spread the paste over the top of each fillet. Drizzle with oil then roast for 15-20 minutes until the crust is golden and the fish cooked. Serve with the sweet potato wedges.

Smoked Salmon Mousse on Rye with Pickled Cucumber and Radish Salad

I never thought I would get the chance to go to Australia, but then I started going out with an Aussie, and of course all that changed. It is a country I am growing to love more and more, not least because of the people I have met there. John does a lot of work with McGuigan Wines and Neil and Debra McGuigan have become real friends. When I asked Deb about her favourite thing to cook she told me that her friends always requested her smoked salmon mousse and she whipped it up for me there and then. It's super easy and is a wonderful light, refreshing lunch – especially under the hot Aussie sun. Double or triple the quantities and serve it as canapés or as a starter for a summer party.

Serves 4

200g smoked salmon
2 tbsp unsalted butter
2 tbsp cream cheese
3 tbsp double cream
1 tbsp capers, finely
    chopped
small bunch of dill, finely
    chopped, plus extra
    sprigs to garnish
good squeeze of lemon juice
4 slices of rye bread
black pepper

For the cucumber and radish salad

1 cucumber
good handful of radishes,
    very finely sliced
120ml rice wine vinegar
2 tbsp caster sugar
2 tsp sea salt
1 tsp fennel seeds

For the salad, peel the cucumber, then use the peeler to make ribbons until you reach the seedy core. Discard the core and put the ribbons in a bowl. Add the radishes very finely and combine with the cucumbers.

In a separate bowl or small jug, mix together the remaining pickling ingredients and pour over the cucumber and radishes. Set aside for about 30 minutes.

In a food processer or blender, briefly blitz the salmon with the butter, cream cheese, cream and capers until you have a rough paste – this isn't a smooth mousse. Spoon into a bowl and stir in the dill and a squeeze of lemon juice until well mixed.

Toast the rye bread, then scoop a nice dollop of mousse on to each slice. Top with the pickled salad, a little sprig of fresh dill and a grind of black pepper.

pictured overleaf ···>

Prawn and Seafood Stick Salad

My friend Katie has featured in my books before, but I couldn't let this recipe go undiscovered. Katie is a fab cook, and with a large Greek family there are always huge family get-togethers and barbecues. She tells me all her friends have asked for this recipe as it goes with pretty much everything! I love a jacket potato for dinner (something that John thinks is very odd!) and this salad makes a great filling for a crispy jacket.

Serves 6 as a starter

bunch of spring onions,
   roughly chopped
I x 250g pack seafood
   sticks, roughly chopped
225g cooked and peeled king
   prawns
handful of coriander,
   chopped
juice of ½ lemon
4 tsp mayonnaise
4 tbsp crème fraîche
salt and pepper

Place the spring onions and seafood sticks into a bowl with the prawns, coriander, lemon juice, mayonnaise and crème fraîche. Season and stir to combine.

Spiced Crab Linguine

This recipe is crying out for a table in the garden, laid out ready for friends to come round and enjoy a light, summery evening meal. It's very quick to make, leaving me plenty of time to sit and chat and enjoy the sunshine.

Serves 4

350g linguine
150g tenderstem broccoli
olive oil
bunch of spring onions,
   finely sliced
I red chilli, finely chopped
200g fresh white crab meat
handful of flat-leaf
   parsley, chopped
lemon juice
extra virgin olive oil
salt and pepper

Cook the pasta in a pan of boiling salted water for 10–12 minutes until al dente.

Meanwhile, blanch the broccoli in boiling water until tender. Drain and refresh under cold water, then slice the stems, keeping the heads whole. Set aside. In a large pan, heat a little oil and fry the spring onions and chilli until translucent and tender.

Add the cooked pasta with a splash of the cooking water to the frying pan, then stir through the broccoli, crab meat, parsley and lemon juice to taste. Season well and tip into a large, warm bowl, drizzle with extra virgin olive oil and serve.

Spicy Sunshine Prawns with Feta Flatbreads

I am always trying to come up with new ideas for my girlfriends when they come over for a meal. Life is so busy nowadays and with all our work and family commitments it's not always easy to see each other, so when my friends do come round I like to make a fuss of them, but I also want to spend time chatting! These spicy prawns are just the ticket. I make the flatbreads in advance and keep them warm in a clean tea towel. If necessary, they can be reheated wrapped in foil in the oven with a few drops of water sprinkled over the top. My one tip is to cook your onions really slowly - the slower the better as they make a real difference to the flavour of the dish.

Serves 6

2 tsp mustard seeds
2 tsp cumin seeds
I tsp coriander seeds
2 tbsp olive oil
I red onion, finely sliced
I red chilli, finely chopped
I garlic clove, crushed
2 tsp garam masala
2 tsp turmeric powder
2 tsp ground coriander
2 tsp sweet smoked paprika
250g cherry tomatoes, halved
250g spinach
250g raw king prawns
grated zest and juice of
    I lemon
bunch of coriander,
    finely chopped
salt and pepper

For the flatbreads
300g self-raising flour
300g natural yoghurt
I tsp baking powder
I tbsp vegetable oil
I00g feta cheese, crumbled

For the flatbreads, mix all the ingredients except for the oil and cheese in a large bowl. Knead to a dough - it's quite a sticky dough - then shape into 6 balls weighing about 50g each and roll them out to about 1cm thick. Brush each bread with the oil, then sprinkle over the feta and fold the dough in on itself (like an envelope) to incorporate the cheese. Use a rolling pin to roll each bread out to about 15cm in diameter (I like small ones).

Heat a griddle or heavy-based frying pan over a medium-high heat until piping hot, then cook the flatbreads for about 30 seconds on each side or until golden (check they're cooked right through).

Place a frying pan over a medium heat and add the mustard, cumin and coriander seeds. Once you start to smell them and the seeds start to pop, add the oil and the onion and cook slowly until the onion is soft and caramelised; this will take a good 10 minutes.

Add the chilli and garlic and cook for a further minute or so. Add the garam masala, turmeric, ground coriander, paprika and 3 tablespoons of water and cook the spices for a minute in the water. Drop in the tomatoes and cook until nice and soft, then add the spinach and cook until wilted. Stir in the prawns and cook until they just turn pink, then season and add a good squeeze of lemon juice and the chopped coriander. Spoon into bowls and serve with the warm flatbreads.

Fish Tacos

I came up with this dish for a children's BBC TV programme called *Crash My Kitchen*. Children would email, phone or write me a letter to tell me what they were bored of eating at home, then give me a list of their favourite ingredients. I'd have to come up with a recipe they liked and then go to their house and teach them how to cook it. I absolutely loved meeting the children, discussing what they liked to cook and helping them to make dishes they were really proud of. These tacos were one of the stand-out recipes for me and the kids. Just leave the chilli out of the salsa if you don't like heat and play around with the other flavours to suit your family's tastes.

Serves 4

75g plain flour
2 medium eggs, beaten
80g panko breadcrumbs
4 cod fillets, approx.
  100-120g each
vegetable oil

For the salsa
1 x 150g tin sweetcorn,
  drained
1 red pepper, finely diced
1 red chilli, deseeded and
  finely diced
4 spring onions, finely
  sliced
½ avocado, cubed
good handful of coriander,
  chopped
juice of 1 lime
1 tbsp olive oil
salt and pepper

To serve
4 large soft flour or corn
  tortillas
shredded lettuce
soured cream

To make the salsa, put the drained sweetcorn into a bowl with the pepper, chilli, onions, avocado and coriander. Add the lime juice and olive oil and mix together. Season to taste and set aside.

Take three shallow bowls and put the flour in one, the beaten eggs in another and the breadcrumbs in the third. Cut the fish fillets in half lengthways and coat them first in the flour, then the egg and finally the breadcrumbs.

Fill a large, deep frying pan with vegetable oil to a depth of around 1cm and place over a medium heat. Test if the oil is hot enough by dropping in a breadcrumb; when it sizzles, it's ready. Cook the fish in the oil for about a minute on each side until the flesh is opaque, then remove from the pan and drain on kitchen towel.

Serve the fish in the flour or corn tortillas, with the lettuce, soured cream and a good dollop of the sweetcorn salsa.

Baked Cod with Chorizo, Chickpeas and Paprika Garlic Sauce

As a mum I'm constantly looking for ways to get Billie to eat fish. I know it's nothing to stress about, but we all want our kids to have a varied diet and fish is something we just inherently know is good for us - it's 'brain food'. Sadly, Billie's really not a fan, but I know she loves chorizo, so we play the bargain game with this dish - she can have a few bits of chorizo but she has to eat the fish, which she then exclaims is 'really nice, Mamma!' If it works for her, you never know, it may work for your children too.

Serves 4

5 tbsp olive oil
200g cooking chorizo,
  chopped
I onion, finely sliced
5 garlic cloves, grated
I tsp sweet smoked paprika
2 tsp sherry vinegar
2 large tbsp dry sherry
500ml chicken or vegetable
  stock
I x 400g tin chickpeas,
  drained and rinsed
4 skinless cod fillets
handful of flat-leaf
  parsley, chopped,
  to serve
salt and pepper

In a medium-sized frying pan, heat 2 teaspoons of oil over a medium heat, add the chorizo chunks and fry until they release their oils. Lift the chorizo out of the pan on to a plate and set aside.

Add the onion to the pan, with another teaspoon of oil, if necessary, and fry until caramelised and really soft. Add the garlic and 3 tablespoons of the remaining oil and cook over a low–medium heat until the garlic has also started to caramelise. Add the paprika, vinegar and sherry and allow to bubble away for a few minutes, then add the stock and seasoning. Continue to cook until reduced a little, then add the chickpeas and the cooked chorizo. Cook for another couple of minutes until warmed through, then set aside and keep warm.

In a non-stick frying pan, heat another tablespoon of oil, then add the cod fillets (placing what would have been the skin side against the pan) and cook for 4–5 minutes until golden and almost cooked through, then flip and cook for a further minute to colour the other side.

Serve the cod in shallow bowls with the chickpeas and garlic sauce spooned over and sprinkled with the parsley.

Lentils and Salmon

Among my friends who are mothers, something we have in common is that we like to share family recipes and talk about what does and doesn't work for our children; it's a conversation I think I have had a million times over. This recipe was given to me by my friend Patsy, who calls it her 'healthy but yummy dinner'. It's packed full of goodness from the fish, vegetables and lentils, and her kids really love it. When you're feeding a family, lentils make a healthy change from pasta or potatoes, but they fill your kids up and most children seem to like their starchy, comforting flavour.

Serves 4

500g Puy lentils
I beef tomato, left whole
3 garlic cloves, unpeeled
few thyme sprigs
I litre vegetable stock
300g spinach
I-2 tbsp crème fraîche
I tsp red wine vinegar
handful of flat-leaf
   parsley, chopped
olive oil
4 salmon fillets
salt and pepper

Rinse the lentils and place them in a large pot with the tomato, garlic and thyme. Pour over the vegetable stock and bring to the boil. Simmer for 20 minutes until the lentils are soft.

Scoop the garlic flesh out the skins, discard the skins, then return the flesh to the lentils along with the spinach. Stir the garlic and spinach into the lentils while also squashing and mashing the tomato (which will have broken down) to mix it in well too. Add the crème fraîche, vinegar and parsley and season well.

Heat a little oil in a non-stick pan over a medium heat and fry the salmon for 3-5 minutes, turning once, until golden brown and just cooked. Serve the salmon with the lentils.

Sunita's Seafood Stew

I met my friend Rosalind after reading her fantastic book called *How I Met My Son*, which is about a mother who, like me, adopted her child. After I read it I had to get in touch with her to tell her what a truly great and inspirational book she had written. We chat when we can and it's nice to know somebody else is in the same sort of boat as I am. Sunita is Roz's best friend and was there for her through those tough early days of the adoption process. Her seafood stew, which her own family absolutely love, has also become a favourite in Roz's house and has now made its way into mine – there's that mothers' network again! Stews are great for families and this one has a good mix of elements – veg and seafood.

Serves 4-6

500g mussels
3 tbsp olive oil
I onion, finely chopped
2 leeks, chopped
2 celery sticks, finely chopped
3 garlic cloves, finely sliced
½ tsp chilli flakes
few sprigs of tarragon
375ml dry white wine
8 fresh tomatoes, chopped
I tbsp sundried tomato paste
600ml fish or vegetable stock
600g mix of cod, smoked haddock and salmon, cut into 3cm chunks
8 large raw prawns
crusty bread, to serve

Place the mussels in a colander in the sink under cold running water. Discard any mussels that are open, and scrub the shells of any that are not, removing the 'beard' that sticks out from the shell if it has one. Set the cleaned mussels aside.

Heat the oil in a large pan, add the onions, leeks, celery, garlic, chilli flakes and tarragon and fry over a medium heat for 15 minutes until lovely and soft. Add the wine and bubble until well reduced.

Add the tomatoes and sundried tomato paste, then reduce the heat and cook until the tomatoes soften – about 5-7 minutes. Add the stock, bring to the boil, then add the fish, prawns and mussels and simmer gently for 5 minutes until the fish is just cooked. Check the seasoning and serve with crusty bread to mop up the juices.

Fish Fritters with Green Salsa

I have a very strong memory of going to my friend Dhruv's house, arriving late after a long drive and particularly starving. He took some lovely crab fritters out of the fridge and heated them up for me and I think I honestly ate the whole lot in about a minute, not even pausing for breath. They were slightly spiced and the flavour I remember is something I still yearn for, so I've taken my memory, played around and have come up with these: a cross between a fritter and a fishcake. Small ones make great canapés, too.

Serves 4

I small cauliflower, broken
    into florets
400g cod fillet
I50g gram flour
I tsp ground turmeric
I tsp ground cumin
2 tsp brown mustard seeds
½ tsp ground coriander
pinch of chilli powder
I00ml sparkling water
vegetable oil
salt and pepper
natural yoghurt, to serve

For the salsa
large bunch of coriander
small bunch of mint
I garlic clove, crushed
2 green finger chillies,
    finely chopped
I small banana shallot,
    finely chopped
juice of I lemon
3 tbsp olive oil

Blanch the cauliflower in boiling salted water for 2–3 minutes, then drain and tip into a bowl.

Place the cod in a fan or bamboo steamer over a pan of simmering water and steam for around 8 minutes until just cooked. Flake the flesh into the bowl with the cauliflower.

In a second bowl, combine the gram flour, spices and a good pinch of salt. Add the sparkling water to make a batter then fold in the flaked fish and cauliflower.

Put all the salsa ingredients into a food processor and blitz to form a coarse paste. Season and set aside.

Heat a good layer of oil in a non-stick frying pan. Fry generous spoonfuls of the fish mixture for 1–2 minutes, turning once, until golden on each side. Drain on kitchen towel then season and serve with natural yoghurt and the salsa.

Salmon Teriyaki

Tamzin Outhwaite has been a friend for years. She was filming *EastEnders* while I was filming *Holby City* and we used to meet in the BBC bar at lunchtime. Those were the days when people still had a drink at lunch! Thinking about it makes me smile; it was quite a funny place to be, with actors in hospital scrubs and dressing gowns all having a pint. Now we have our children and our families and life is a little different. Tamzin and her family love this recipe as it's really quick and healthy, and the leftover salmon is also good cold, mixed into a salad for lunchboxes. The sticky rice 'cakes' are my addition. I'm not a huge fan of rice but wanted to try and entice myself so came up with these – they are fun, gooey, with a hint of sweetness and are a delicious way of eating rice.

Serves 4

100ml mirin
100ml soy sauce
100ml sake
70g caster sugar
500g piece of salmon fillet
1 tbsp groundnut oil

For the sticky rice cakes

240g sushi rice
720ml water
2 tbsp vegetable oil
bunch of spring onions,
   finely chopped
2cm piece of ginger, grated
2 tbsp rice vinegar
1 tsp mirin
1 tbsp sesame oil
salt and pepper

In a pan, heat the mirin, soy sauce, sake and sugar over a low heat until the sugar melts, then increase the heat and allow the liquid to bubble until it becomes lovely and sticky. Leave to cool then place the salmon in a shallow bowl, pour over the marinade and set aside.

For the rice cakes, put the rice in a small, heavy-bottomed pan and add the water. Cover the pan with a lid; for best results, do not uncover it at any time during cooking. Bring to a boil over a medium-high heat and leave to boil for 4–5 minutes. (If you don't have a clear saucepan lid you will have to listen to the pan to hear it bubbling, or it's fine to take a very quick look!) Reduce the heat to low and simmer, covered, for 10 minutes. Remove the pan from the heat and let the rice stand, covered, for 15 minutes. When you lift the lid, all the liquid should have been absorbed. Leave the rice to cool a little so you can shape it with your hands (it may be soft).

Heat 1 tablespoon of the vegetable oil in a frying pan, then add the spring onions and ginger and cook on a low heat until softened. Add these to the rice along with the rice vinegar, mirin and some salt and pepper. Shape the rice into cakes about 5cm wide and set aside on baking paper in the fridge until you are ready to fry them.

For the greens

I tbsp groundnut oil

I red chilli, finely chopped

2 garlic cloves, finely
   chopped

400g choi sum or pak choi
   (or a mix)

I tbsp soy sauce

2 tsp sesame oil

I tbsp toasted sesame seeds

To cook the salmon, heat the groundnut oil in a large frying pan over a medium heat and fry the salmon in its teriyaki marinade for 4–5 minutes on each side, until just cooked and really sticky and charred on the outside. Set aside to rest.

Meanwhile, for the rice cakes, heat the remaining vegetable oil and the sesame oil in a separate frying pan and fry the cakes for 2–3 minutes on one side until they have a good golden crust, then flip and cook them until golden on the other side. Transfer to a serving plate.

For the greens, heat the groundnut oil in a wok over a high heat and stir-fry the chilli and garlic for a few seconds. Add the greens and a splash of water and cook quickly until the greens have wilted and softened, then add the soy sauce, sesame oil and half the sesame seeds.

Spoon on to a serving dish, place the salmon on top and scatter with the remaining sesame seeds. Serve with the rice cakes.

pictured overleaf ···>

PATSY O'NEILL

Lentils and Salmon

ROSALIND POWELL

Sunita's Seafood Stew

DEBRA MCGUIGAN

**Smoked Salmon Mousse
with Pickled Cucumber
and Salad**

KATIE LIASIS

**Prawn and Seafood
Stick Salad**

DHRUV BAKER

Fish Fritters

TAMZIN OUTHWAITE

Salmon Teriyaki

******

'Among my friends who are
mothers, we like to share
family recipes and talk
about what does and doesn't
work for our children; it's a
conversation I think I have
had a million times over.'

VEGGIES

✱ ✱ ✱ ✱ ✱ ✱

Courgette, Pea and Dill Soup

Tortilla Chip Soup

Black-eyed Bean Salad

Spicy Baked Eggs

Asparagus and Pesto Tart

Carrot and Pecorino Fritters

Green Bean and Sesame Noodles

Pat's Quick Mushroom Tagliatelle

Linguine Bake with Aubergine, Vine Tomatoes
and Mozzarella

Fagi

Spanish Omelette

Cowboy Beans

Broccoli Pasta

Welsh Potato and Onion Bake

Zucchini Slice

Mac and Cheese with Squash Béchamel

Sweet Potato, Chickpea and Spinach Curry

Leek, Squash and Blue Cheese Pithivier

Thatched Cottage Pie

Kale Frittata

Lentil and Split Pea Bake

Paneer Curry Skewers

Courgette, Pea and Dill Soup

This is a mixture of two recipes, one from my godmother Ann who loves peas, and the other from my friend Victoria. It's a lovely light spring soup, which sits just as well on a dinner party menu as in a flask on a walk!

Serves 4

30g unsalted butter
I onion, sliced
I garlic clove, smashed
2–3 courgettes, grated
I–2 floury potatoes, diced
300g frozen petit pois
I litre vegetable stock
I heaped tsp dill
squeeze of lemon juice
curd cheese or crème
   fraîche (optional)
salt and pepper

Melt the butter in a frying pan over a low heat, add the onion and soften gently for 5-10 minutes, then add the smashed garlic clove and courgette and sauté for 5 minutes. Add the potatoes, peas and stock and simmer for 20 minutes until the potatoes are cooked through.

In a food processor or using a stick blender, blend the soup to the desired consistency, adding a little more stock or hot water if necessary, then stir through the chopped dill and a squeeze of lemon juice and season to taste.

Spoon into bowls with a dollop of curd cheese or crème fraîche, if desired.

Tortilla Chip Soup

Angela Griffin is my best friend. I adore her and everything she is. She loves food and cooking, and she and her husband Jasee make the most delicious dinners so I love going round to their house. They like to do meat-free Mondays and on one occasion she came up with this soup, which is basically a meal in a bowl as the tortilla chips thicken it.

Serves 4-6

I tbsp olive oil
2 onions, sliced
2 garlic cloves, grated
I tbsp chipotle paste
I.5 litres vegetable stock
2 x 400g tins chopped
  tomatoes
I tbsp soft brown sugar
I tsp dried oregano
I x 200g bag of plain
  tortilla chips
I x 200g tin sweetcorn,
  drained

To serve
Cheddar cheese, grated
chopped coriander
soured cream

Heat the oil in a large pan over a low heat, add the onion and soften slowly for about 10 minutes until lovely and sweet. Add the garlic and cook for another 3-4 minutes until soft, then add the chipotle paste and a splash of stock and heat through. Add the tomatoes, sugar, oregano, a handful of tortilla chips and the remaining stock and cook for about 30 minutes, until thick and soupy.

Using a stick blender or food processor, blitz the soup and transfer back to the pan. Add the sweetcorn and heat through.

Spoon into large bowls, crushing some tortilla chips into each one and sprinkling with Cheddar cheese, coriander and a dollop of soured cream.

Black-eyed Bean Salad

My daughter Billie's sports day is always a really nice excuse for mums and dads to get together and have a natter while we cheer our monkeys on! Everybody brings a picnic and after the sports all the children and their families sit down and share them. I usually make something like sausage rolls or my Energy Balls (see page 215), but my mum friend Vidushi once brought this scrumptious salad. I ended up eating most of it so I then pestered her for the recipe. I now make this a lot in the summer, in batches, and every time I take a trip to the fridge for something I start eating it out the container.

Serves 6-8

2 x 400g tins black-eyed
  beans
220g cherry tomatoes,
  quartered
½ cucumber, cubed
handful of radishes, thinly
  sliced
I avocado, cubed
I tbsp chopped coriander
I tbsp chopped mint
juice of ½ lemon
salt and pepper

In a large bowl, combine the beans with the remaining ingredients and a good grind of salt and pepper.

Serve this as a side or on its own. I store it in a plastic container in the fridge for a day and it's a regular in Billie's packed lunch.

Spicy Baked Eggs

I have become slightly obsessed with this of late - I don't think there is anything not to love about tomatoes, eggs and a little bit of spice, all mopped up with bread. There is a restaurant not far from where I live that does the best version served with fresh, hot, fluffy pitas, and this is my attempt to recreate it at home. If you want to make your own pittas or flatbreads, they're so easy - turn to page 79 or 107 for my recipes.

Serves 4

75ml olive oil
2 onions, finely sliced
2 red peppers, finely sliced
3 garlic cloves, crushed
2 tsp cumin seeds
I tbsp smoked sweet paprika
good pinch of cayenne
  pepper
2 x 400g tins chopped
  tomatoes
2 tsp caster sugar
2 tsp red wine vinegar
few thyme sprigs
I bay leaf
4 eggs
large handful of coriander,
  chopped
salt and pepper
Greek yoghurt, to serve
pittas, flatbreads or
  baguette, to serve

Heat the oil in a wide, shallow pan with a lid and gently fry the onions over a low heat for 10 minutes, then add the peppers and fry for a further 5-6 minutes until both are lovely and soft.

Add the garlic and spices and cook for 2-3 minutes, then pour in the tomatoes. Add the sugar and vinegar, thyme, bay leaf and plenty of seasoning and simmer gently for around 30 minutes until the sauce is thickened.

Make 4 wells in the sauce and break an egg into each one. Cover with a lid then cook for 6-8 minutes over the lowest heat possible until the eggs are just set but the yolks still runny. Sprinkle with coriander and serve with Greek yoghurt and plenty of pittas, flatbreads or crusty baguette.

Asparagus and Pesto Tart

My beautiful niece Lucy and her mother Lou came up with this recipe. I love that they cook together – I know from cooking with Billie how much that bond is strengthened even more through doing something together. Billie and I make heart-shaped versions of these tarts, which look extra pretty!

Serves 4-6

375g ready-rolled sheet all-
   butter puff pastry
bunch of asparagus
2 tbsp fresh pesto
2 tbsp crème fraîche
I tbsp cream cheese
I00g firm mozzarella,
   grated
25g pine nuts
I egg, beaten
olive oil
salt and pepper
basil, to serve (optional)

Heat the oven to 200°C/gas 6.

Unroll the pastry and place on a baking tray. Score a border around 2cm from the edge and prick inside the border with a fork. Bake for 15 minutes until lightly golden and puffed up, then remove from the oven and push down the centre of the tart.

Meanwhile, blanch the asparagus in boiling water for 2 minutes, then drain and cool under cold running water. Cut each spear in half lengthways.

In a bowl, mix the pesto with the crème fraîche and cream cheese and season well. Spread this over the base of the pastry and top with the sliced asparagus, then sprinkle with the grated mozzarella and pine nuts. Brush the edge of the pastry with beaten egg, then return to the oven for 10 minutes until the cheese is melted and the edges golden.

Drizzle with oil, scatter with basil leaves and serve.

Carrot and Pecorino Fritters

While cooking several meal options can sound like a bit of a hassle, John and I have really wanted to embrace my extended family's decision to become vegetarian and we've enjoyed the challenge of coming up with interesting new things to make when they drop in for dinner. These fritters are something I devised one evening. I used vegetarian Parmesan for my nieces as they don't eat pecorino due to the rennet, but pecorino is a lovely alternative for those who do. Serve these simply with natural yoghurt and green vegetables or a salad.

Serves 4

2 tbsp olive oil
2 shallots, finely sliced
I garlic clove, grated
225g grated carrot
I25g grated squash or
    potato
I tsp fennel seeds
zest of ½ lemon
80g grated pecorino cheese
    (or vegetarian alternative)
I00g plain flour
½ tsp white pepper
salt

Heat the oil in a frying pan over a low heat, add the shallots and fry for 5 minutes to gently soften. Add the garlic and cook for a further 3-4 minutes until soft.

In a bowl, combine the cooked shallots and garlic with the carrot, squash, herbs and lemon zest.

In a separate bowl, mix the pecorino with the flour, some salt and the white pepper, then add this to the grated carrot mix and bring everything together with your hands.

Take 1 tablespoon of the mix and shape it into a patty. Repeat with the remaining mixture; you should get about 10 in total.

Heat 0.5cm oil in a frying pan and cook the fritters in batches for about 5 minutes until browned on each side. Drain on kitchen towel and serve.

Green Bean and Sesame Noodles

As a member of the band All Saints, my friend Natalie is so busy that she rarely has time for cooking. However, when we were chatting about what to feed our children she said that she and her family love green beans and sesame noodles, so, for Natalie, here are the best noodles I could muster. Delicious hot out of the pan, they're also brilliant cold in kids' lunchboxes.

Serves 2-3

200g dried egg noodles
I20g green beans
3 tbsp soy sauce
3 tbsp sesame oil
2 tbsp mirin
I garlic clove, grated
Icm piece of ginger, grated
6 spring onions, finely
    sliced
I-2 tbsp sesame seeds

Cook the noodles according to the packet instructions.

Blanch the green beans for 1 minute in a pan of boiling water, then drain and set aside.

In a bowl, whisk together the soy sauce, 2 tablespoons sesame oil, mirin, garlic and ginger.

In a large frying pan, heat the remaining sesame oil and add the spring onions. Fry until softened, then add the noodles, beans and sauce, heat through, then sprinkle with the sesame seeds and serve.

Pat's Quick Mushroom Tagliatelle

My godmother Pat used to make these creamy mushrooms and serve them on toast as a starter when my mum and dad came over for dinner. I have been using it as a pasta sauce because it's such a quick and easy family supper and is simply delicious.

Serves 4

300g **tagliatelle**
olive oil
50g **unsalted butter**
2 **banana shallots, sliced**
I **garlic clove, grated**
300g **mushrooms, sliced**
few **thyme sprigs**
I00g **crème fraîche**
½ tsp **Dijon mustard**
salt and pepper

Bring a large pan of water to the boil. Add the pasta with a pinch of salt and a glug of olive oil and cook according to the packet instructions.

Meanwhile, melt the butter in a pan over a medium heat, add the shallots and cook for about 5 minutes until starting to soften. Add the garlic, toss in the mushrooms and thyme sprigs and cook for 3–4 minutes until the mushrooms have softened. Pour in the crème fraîche and mustard, mix well and season to taste.

Drain the pasta and add to the sauce. Stir to combine until the pasta is well coated in sauce and serve.

Linguine Bake with Aubergine, Vine Tomatoes and Mozzarella

A pasta bake may not be the most original of dishes, but I think it's something that needs to be in every mum's repertoire as it's such a good fallback and in my experience never fails to get a smile. This is my family's favourite – Billie usually has third helpings so I had to include it.

Serves 4

2 aubergines
I red onion, cut into wedges
400g vine tomatoes,
   quartered
I–2 garlic cloves, smashed
few thyme or rosemary
   sprigs
5 tbsp olive oil
350g linguine
I50ml vegetable stock or
   pasta cooking water
200ml passata
I x large mozzarella ball,
   torn into pieces
large handful of pitted
   green olives
25g grated Parmesan
large handful of
   breadcrumbs, fresh or
   dried
salt and pepper

Heat the oven to 200°C/gas 6.

Cut the aubergines into bite-sized pieces and place in a roasting tin with the onions, tomatoes, garlic and herbs. Season well, drizzle with the oil, then toss everything together and roast for 45 minutes until really soft and tender.

Towards the end of the roasting time, cook the linguine in boiling salted water for 8 minutes until al dente. Drain the pasta, retaining the cooking water, and return to the pan with the stock or cooking water and the passata. Tip the roasted veg into the pan and stir to combine.

Tip the pasta and veg into a 23 x 30cm ovenproof dish and dot all over with the mozzarella and olives, nestling them into the pasta. Scatter with Parmesan and breadcrumbs and bake in the oven for 10 minutes until golden brown and the cheese is melting and oozy. I actually like to cook mine a little longer so that some of the pasta is crispy on top. Serve alongside a green salad.

pictured overleaf ••• >

Fagi

This is a fantastic lentil dish from my Greek friend Andri. In the Greek Orthodox Church, the week before Easter is considered a fast week and they have to abstain from eating meat, fish, dairy and poultry. Despite that, when she tells me about her Easter family gatherings it sounds like the table is literally groaning with food and I am desperate to be invited so that I can see it for myself. This simple, hearty dish often crops up as it's filling yet flavoursome. You'll need to serve it with a couple of other vegetable dishes or mezze to turn it into a complete meal, but that's easily done with some crunchy raw vegetables, pots of hummus and a simple Greek salad, or if you're not just catering for vegetarians, the Koftas recipe on page 79.

Serves 4 (as a side)

250g green lentils
I vegetable stock cube
I00g basmati rice
2 tbsp olive oil
2 onions, finely sliced
2 garlic cloves, crushed
juice of ½ lemon
salt and pepper

Put the lentils in a pan of water, bring to the boil and simmer for 10 minutes, then drain and return to the pan with the stock cube. Cover the lentils with water, to about 5cm above the top of the lentils, and bring to the boil then simmer for 5 minutes. Add the rice and simmer until both are cooked and the liquid absorbed, about 15 minutes.

Meanwhile, heat the oil in a pan over a low heat and gently fry the onions for 10-15 minutes until soft and golden, adding the garlic for the last 2 minutes.

Once the rice and lentils are cooked, remove from the heat, stir in the lemon juice, onions and seasoning, then cover and stand for 10 minutes before serving.

Spanish Omelette

My sister Victoria's friend and neighbour Maite is Spanish, and she taught me and Victoria how to make a proper Spanish omelette. It's such a staple in households that, like all Spanish families, her mother always has the ingredients to hand. When Maite used to visit her grandparents in Catalonia, her grandmother would make one in no time at all, and at 95 still manages to have the potatoes and onions frying in the pan in what seems like seconds. What is amazing is how she peels and slices the potatoes and onions without using a chopping board; she does it all above the frying pan. I haven't managed to master that yet, but boy is this a good omelette.

Serves 4

400g waxy potatoes, sliced
    to around 0.5cm thickness
olive oil
I onion, halved and thinly
    sliced
6 large eggs
salt
crusty bread, to serve

Dry the potato slices on kitchen towel or in a clean tea towel. Heat a good glug of oil in a 16cm lidded frying pan over a medium heat, and when hot add the potatoes and onions and stir. Turn the heat to low, cover and cook for 20-30 minutes. Check regularly that they are not burning and stir occasionally to prevent sticking and to ensure even cooking. The potatoes are completely cooked when they feel soft when pricked with a sharp knife.

While the potatoes are cooking, beat the eggs together in a large bowl. Take the frying pan off the heat and, using a slotted spoon, add the potatoes and onions to the eggs and combine gently, adding a large pinch of salt. Put the frying pan back over a medium heat, add extra oil if needed and, once the oil is hot, turn the heat to low and add the potato and egg mixture.

Cook for around 4 minutes until the underside is golden brown; you can check this by putting a fork between the mixture and the side of the frying pan and slightly raising the omelette to see the underside. Once brown you need to carefully flip the omelette over to cook the other side. Take a flat plate that is larger than the frying pan, remove the pan from the heat, put the plate over the top of the frying pan and carefully flip it on to the plate - the quicker you do this, the less likely it is to go wrong!

Add another glug of oil to the pan and heat, then slide the omelette back into the pan. Cook for a further 4-5 minutes until golden brown, then slide on to a plate, slice and serve with crusty bread.

Cowboy Beans

My friend Olivia is a mum of two and a GP. She is really busy but super organised. She has a few staple dishes she makes for her veggie/vegan/carnivorous family, and this is one that suits them all. It is also a perfect dish to have bubbling away on the stove, so that when family members get in from school, clubs and work at different times it's ready to go. Olivia always buys dried beans and soaks them overnight, but the truth is I don't always remember to do that so I just use tinned beans, which work really well.

Serves 4-6

2 tbsp olive oil
I red onion, finely sliced
2 garlic cloves, crushed
I x 400g tin chopped
   tomatoes
I x 300g jar fresh tomato
   salsa
I tsp hot smoked paprika
300ml water
I x 400g tin kidney beans,
   drained and rinsed
I x 400g tin pinto or turtle
   beans, drained and rinsed
I x 400g black beans,
   drained and rinsed
salt and pepper

To serve
brown rice
sliced avocado
grated cheese, such as
   Cheddar

Heat the oil in a large casserole, add the onion and fry over a low heat for 20-25 minutes until softened and sticky. Add the garlic and fry for another minute, then add the tomatoes, salsa, paprika and water. Season and allow to bubble over a low heat, with the lid partially on, for 40 minutes, adding a splash more water if it starts to look dry.

Add the beans and cook for a further 10 minutes, then serve with brown rice, avocado slices and grated cheese.

Broccoli Pasta

I am very fortunate in my line of work to meet actresses that I really admire. When I first met Julie Graham I was slightly star-struck and just had to go up to her and tell her how amazing I thought she was; I think I may have scared her slightly! We chatted a little about our families and she said to me that although she wasn't a huge fan of cooking, her girls did like broccoli pasta, which by chance is also a huge hit in my house. So, beautiful Julie – this recipe is for you and your children.

Billie loves chilli, but not all children do so you can just leave it out if yours aren't fans. And I know some people would worry about children not liking anchovies, but I promise you they're just a good way of getting salt into the dish - if you don't tell them there are anchovies, they won't know! Just be careful with the quantity - any more than I've suggested and it does start to have a fishy flavour.

Serves 4

olive oil
6 spring onions, finely
  sliced
I garlic clove, grated
I red chilli, finely chopped
6 anchovy fillets, rinsed
250g tenderstem broccoli,
  halved crossways
handful of halved cherry
  tomatoes
350g short pasta shapes
salt and pepper
Parmesan, grated, to serve

Heat the oven to 180°C/gas 4.

Heat a good glug of olive oil in an ovenproof frying pan or saucepan over a medium heat. Add the spring onions and fry for a few minutes to soften a little, then add the garlic and chilli and fry for a further minute until softened.

Add the anchovies and let them melt into the oil, then remove from the heat and toss through the broccoli, tomatoes and seasoning, making sure the broccoli is coated in the chilli. Place in the oven for about 5 minutes or so.

Meanwhile, bring a pan of water to the boil, add the pasta and cook according to the packet instructions. Drain but reserve a little of the cooking water. Add the pasta to the broccoli with a splash of the water to loosen the sauce and give everything a good mix. Serve with lots of grated Parmesan and black pepper.

Welsh Potato and Onion Bake

A traditional Welsh recipe that is comfort food at its simplest – thin layers of potato and onion baked in the oven until soft and sticky. This version comes from my friend Hayley's grandmother who is Welsh, but I have a similar recipe and have merged the two. Although it's great as a side for lamb or beef, I will happily eat this with a spoon straight from the baking dish or with a fried egg on top.

Serves 6 as a side

50g unsalted butter, plus
   extra for greasing
500g onion, finely sliced
6 thyme sprigs
1kg floury potatoes, peeled
   and thinly sliced
salt and pepper

Heat the oven to 200°C/gas 6.

Melt a knob of the butter in a pan over a low heat and fry the onions gently for 10-15 minutes until soft.

Grease a 25 x 15cm ovenproof dish with a little butter. Melt the remaining butter in a large pan, add the thyme and season well. Add the potatoes and onions and toss with the melted butter, then arrange them in layers in the dish. Once all the potatoes and onions are layered, press down firmly with a spatula, then bake in the oven for 45 minutes until golden and crispy.

Zucchini Slice

John's Auntie Mary is one of my favourite people. On my first trip to Australia she sat me down and showed me photos of John as a boy, and the next time I went over there I drove to her house while John was working and sat with her for hours looking at old family photos and hearing stories about John's childhood. Auntie Mary makes her Zucchini Slice for all the family get-togethers. It is sort of a quiche with no base and it's great hot or cold, so perfect for a gathering. The first time I tried it I took a wedge back to our hotel room and scoffed it at 4am, bug-eyed and starving thanks to jetlag – it was so good!

Serves 6

400g courgettes, grated
100g Cheddar cheese, grated
    plus extra for sprinkling
    (optional)
4 tbsp olive oil
150g self-raising flour
I large onion, finely sliced
5 medium eggs, beaten
30g fresh breadcrumbs
salt and pepper

Heat the oven to 180°C/gas 4. Line a 23cm springform cake tin with non-stick baking paper.

In a bowl, combine all the ingredients except the breadcrumbs and pour into the prepared tin. Sprinkle with the breadcrumbs and a little more cheese for that extra crunch, if you wish.

Place in the oven for 30-40 minutes until golden and firm on top, but still with a little spring to it, then slice and serve.

Mac and Cheese with Squash Béchamel

I met Lizzie when she was working at *delicious.* magazine and I was writing my first book. We really hit it off and a a close friendship blossomed. Now, for this book, I've finally had the joy of working with her. It was Lizzie who came up with the genius idea of adding squash to a béchamel and I now cook it on a regular basis. It's such a great one for children because from a mum's point of view it's an ideal way of sneaking extra veg into their meals without them knowing.

Serves 4

500g butternut squash,
    chopped
350ml semi-skimmed milk
75ml double cream
grating of nutmeg
250g macaroni
olive oil
I onion, sliced
I tsp English mustard
    powder
200g strong Cheddar cheese,
    grated
30g Parmesan, grated
salt and pepper

Heat the oven to 200°C/gas 6.

Put the squash in a pan and cover with the milk, bring to a simmer and cook for 10-12 minutes until tender. Blend to a purée with a stick blender then add the cream, nutmeg and plenty of seasoning.

Tip the macaroni into a pan of boiling salted water and cook for 6 minutes until starting to become tender but still firm. Drain, retaining a little of the cooking water, and toss with a little oil and a splash of the water to stop it sticking.

Heat a little more oil in a frying pan over a low heat and gently fry the onion for 10 minutes until softened. Stir in the mustard powder, then add the cooked onion to the butternut squash purée. Stir in the Cheddar and the macaroni, check the seasoning and tip into a 1.2-litre ovenproof dish. Sprinkle with the Parmesan and bake in the oven for 15-20 minutes until golden on top. Leave to stand for 10 minutes before serving.

Sweet Potato, Chickpea & Spinach Curry

My sister Victoria and I are very close. She lives round the corner from me and our families often eat together as we're constantly at each other's houses. Victoria stopped eating meat a couple of years ago and my two nieces have now joined her - one of them is vegan. This can prove challenging at meal times when there are also two meat eaters in the house, however one meal that everybody loves is a vegetable curry.

This recipe started off as a basic chickpea and spinach curry, but the more Victoria and I cooked it, sometimes adding other veg, we realised that potatoes were our favourite part. One day I decided to try tinned potatoes as a time-saver and everybody is now converted. The texture is much better as they don't overcook and disintegrate the way fresh potatoes can. Although it takes a while to chop the veg, this keeps for ages in the fridge and freezer so I make it in big batches. Our girls eat it the next day for lunch and then for dinner again a few days later. It is their favourite meal now and they request it again and again. We serve it with a tomato, cucumber and onion salad, rice, natural yoghurt (or soy yoghurt) and poppadoms.

Serves 4-6

2 sweet potatoes, about 500g, chopped into large chunks
vegetable oil
2 red onions, sliced
4 tbsp rogan josh curry paste
I red chilli, finely chopped
3cm piece of ginger, grated
2 x 300g tins new potatoes, drained and cut into halves or quarters
2 courgettes, chopped into chunks
I x 400g tin chickpeas, drained and rinsed
6-8 ripe tomatoes, chopped into large chunks
I x 400g tin chopped tomatoes
I x 400ml tin coconut milk
250g spinach

Heat the oven to 200°C/gas 6.

Place the sweet potato on a baking tray, drizzle with oil and cook in the oven for around 15 minutes to soften.

Heat 2 tablespoons of vegetable oil in a large casserole or deep frying pan over a medium heat. Add the onions and curry paste and stir well, cooking until the onions are soft.

Add the chilli, ginger, potatoes and sweet potato, cook for 6 minutes, then add the courgettes and chickpeas. Stir to combine and cook for 6-8 minutes until the courgettes are softened. Add the fresh and tinned tomatoes, then fill the tin with water and pour that in as well. Give the curry a good stir and let it simmer uncovered for about 30 minutes until the sauce starts to thicken. Add the coconut milk and continue cooking for about 5 minutes until you have a thick sauce.

Add the spinach leaves and leave to cook until the spinach is wilted.

Leek, Squash and Blue Cheese Pithivier

A pithivier is a free-form pie originating from the town of Pithiviers in central France, characterised by the Catherine wheel pattern that is usually scored into the top of the pastry. The original is sweet – made from almonds – but pithiviers can now be filled with whatever the cook wants. As soon as I learned how to make one I went on a mission and tried all sorts of different versions, but this one was the winner. I think I've achieved the perfect ratio of filling to pastry and the gorgonzola flavour isn't too strong. I hope you agree. Be careful when scoring your pastry not to cut too deeply as the filling will burst through and ruin its prettiness. This is one of those dishes that looks a lot more complicated than it actually is and everyone thinks you've slaved for hours.

Serves 6

½ butternut squash, peeled
  and cut into Icm cubes
2 tbsp olive oil
60g unsalted butter
3 small leeks, sliced
few thyme sprigs, leaves
  only
I20g crème fraîche
80-I00g gorgonzola
  (depending how cheesy you
  want it!)
500g ready made puff pastry
  (but not ready-rolled)
I egg, beaten
salt and pepper

Heat the oven to 180°C/gas 4. Line a baking tray with non-stick baking paper.

Toss the butternut squash cubes with the olive oil in a roasting tin and roast in the oven for around 30 minutes until tender. Remove from the oven and leave to cool. Increase the oven temperature to 200°C/gas 6.

Melt half the butter in a pan over a low-medium heat and add the sliced leeks. When they start to soften and colour, add 2 tablespoons of water and the remaining butter. Cover and cook for a further 10–15 minutes until tender. Remove the lid and let the leeks cook for another 3–4 minutes until the liquid has evaporated. Set aside to cool.

In a bowl, gently mix together the squash, leeks and thyme leaves with the crème fraîche, then crumble in the gorgonzola and season to taste.

Roll half the pastry out on a floured worktop into a 25cm round. Place on the lined tray. Leaving a 2.5cm margin around the edge, fill the disc with the filling, then egg wash the edge.

Roll out another disc of pastry to a diameter of 35cm and press down on to the filling so it resembles a hat. Fork the edges to seal. Using a sharp knife, very carefully score a 'Catherine wheel' shape from the centre. Trim the edges, egg wash all over and set aside in the fridge for 20 minutes.

Place in the oven for 10 minutes before turning the heat down to 180°C/gas 4 and cooking for a further 30 minutes, until risen and golden. Leave the pithivier to stand for 10–15 minutes before cutting into wedges.

This is also delicious served cold so any leftovers are great wrapped up in foil and popped into your or your little ones' lunchboxes.

pictured overleaf ••• >

Thatched Cottage Pie

This comes from my lovely friend Sarah, who is vegetarian and lives in a thatched cottage. It is an easy, dependable recipe for a vegetarian twist on the classic pie; I have made it many times and it is now a confirmed staple in my house.

Serves 4-6

I tbsp olive oil
½ onion, finely chopped
2 large carrots, chopped
2 garlic cloves, finely
   chopped
a few thyme sprigs, leaves
   stripped
I x 400g tin chopped
   tomatoes
300ml vegetable stock
I generous tsp Marmite
I x 400g tin green lentils,
   drained and rinsed
I x 400g tin cannellini
   beans, drained and rinsed
I x 400g tin butter beans,
   drained and rinsed
I tbsp ketchup
I tsp Dijon mustard
400g sweet potato, chopped
into 3cm chunks
400g Desiree or Vivaldi
   potatoes, chopped into
3cm chunks
25g unsalted butter
50g Cheddar cheese
salt and pepper

Heat the oven to 200°C/gas 6.

Heat the oil in a large pan, add the onion and fry over a medium heat for around 10 minutes until golden. Add the carrots, garlic and the thyme, fry for 1 minute then pour in the tomatoes, stock and Marmite and simmer for 10 minutes. Add the lentils and beans, the ketchup and mustard. Season generously and simmer for a further 10 minutes.

Meanwhile, cook the sweet potato and potatoes in a pan of boiling salted water for around 20 minutes until soft, then mash with the butter.

Pour the filling into a 1.5-litre ovenproof dish and top with the mash. Sprinkle the cheese over and pop it in the oven for about 30 minutes, until golden and bubbling.

Kale Frittata

I have been practising yoga for nearly 20 years – it's one of the only 'sporty' things that I love – and my yoga teacher Nadia has become a good friend. Nadia's sister Katia is a great cook and runs the Nectar Café at triyoga's Camden studio in London, making the most healthy and delicious food. Though I'm not hugely into 'clean eating' as a general rule, Katia's food has converted me a little, it is sooo tasty as well as being super healthy. This frittata is something she makes for her family on a regular basis and I now make it for mine too.

Serves 8-9

I tbsp olive oil
I red onion, finely sliced
200g sweet potato, cut into
   I.5cm cubes
200g kale, thick stems
   removed, shredded
I2 medium eggs
I tsp salt
I tsp baking powder

Heat the oven to 180°C/gas 4.

Heat the oil in a large non-stick pan over a low heat and fry the onion gently for 10 minutes. Add the sweet potato and kale and a splash of water and cook for another 5-10 minutes until the kale is softened and the sweet potato tender.

In a large bowl, beat the eggs with the salt and baking powder. Add the sweet potato and kale mix to the egg and stir to combine.

Line a 20cm square baking tray with baking parchment. Pour the frittata mixture into the tray and bake in the oven for around 25 minutes until golden and set. Remove from the tin and cut into squares.

Lentil and Split Pea Bake

Because of the changing diets of my extended family, it's becoming increasingly important for me and my sister to be able to make a simple, wholesome vegetarian dish that can also work alongside a roast chicken, a side of salmon or tray of sausages for the meat eaters. This bake makes a versatile centerpiece on its own served with some green veg, but also works as a simple side for meat. My tip is to take your time cooking the onions and leeks as it really does make a difference to the flavour of the bake.

Serves 6

200g red lentils
100g yellow split peas
80g unsalted butter, plus
   extra for greasing
2 onions, sliced
2 leeks, sliced
1 garlic clove, grated
2–3 thyme sprigs, leaves
   only
2 large tsp Marmite
200ml water or vegetable
   stock
200g Cheddar cheese, grated
good handful of fresh
   breadcrumbs
salt and pepper

Heat the oven to 190°C/gas 5 and grease a 20 x 25cm baking dish with butter.

Wash the lentils and place them in a bowl, cover with cold water and soak for 15 minutes, then drain. Meanwhile, wash the split peas and put them into a saucepan with 500ml of water. Bring to the boil, then lower the heat and simmer for 15 minutes. Drain.

Melt the butter in a large frying pan over a low heat and cook the onions and leeks slowly for around 10 minutes until almost softened. Add the garlic and cook for another couple of minutes, until everything is soft and starting to colour. Add the soaked lentils and cooked split peas, thyme, Marmite, water or stock and seasoning, then remove from the heat and stir in all but a handful of the Cheddar.

Spoon the mixture into the baking dish, sprinkle over the remaining cheese and the breadcrumbs and bake in the oven for around 40 minutes, until golden and bubbling on top and caramelised around the edges.

Paneer Curry Skewers

With an Aussie boyfriend, barbecues are very popular at my house, but given the increasing number of vegetarians in the family I need to find inventive new things to pop on the grill for them. I have a little bit of a love affair going on with paneer – the mild-flavoured Indian cheese – so these skewers are perfect. Paneer is a firm cheese so can hold up well to being stuck on a stick; the only problem is that I now have to make double as everybody wants them!

Serves 2

2 large tbsp tikka curry
  paste
250g Greek yoghurt
handful of coriander,
  chopped
I tbsp chopped mint
  leaves
250g paneer, cut into 2cm
  cubes
I courgette
8 cherry tomatoes
I tbsp olive oil
flatbreads, to serve

In a bowl, combine the tikka paste with the yoghurt and the herbs. Add the paneer and coat in the yoghurt marinade. Cover and leave in the fridge for several hours or ideally overnight.

Soak 8 wooden skewers in warm water for an hour or so to prevent them burning, or use metal skewers. Heat a barbecue until good and hot.

Using a vegetable peeler, slice the courgette into long strips. Place in a bowl and toss with the cherry tomatoes and the oil. Thread the paneer (retaining any leftover marinade), courgette and cherry tomatoes on to the skewers.

Cook on the barbecue for about 2 minutes each side, spooning over a little extra yoghurt marinade if desired, and serve with flatbreads and a dollop of any leftover marinade.

ANDRI LANITIS

Fagi

MAITE BERNDES

Spanish Omelette

OLIVIA MUNN

Cowboy Beans

JULIE GRAHAM

Broccoli Pasta

ANGELA GRIFFIN

Tortilla Chip Soup

KATIA PHILLIPS

Kale Frittata

VICTORIA SCRIVEN

Sweet Potato and
Chickpea Curry

SARAH FREETHY

Thatched Cottage Pie

HAYLEY CLAPHAM

Welsh Potato &
Onion Bake

PAT FARMILOE

Quick Mushroom
Tagliatelle

LOUISE PEARSON

Asparagus and Pesto Tart

AUNTIE MARY

Zucchini Slice

NATALIE APPLETON

Green Bean &
Sesame Noodles

LIZZIE KAMENETZKY

Mac & Cheese with
Squash Béchamel

VIDUSHI PATEL

Black-eyed Bean Salad

SWEET

✴✴✴✴✴✴

Lemon and Raspberry Brioche Bread and Butter Pudding

Chocolate and Coconut Torte

Farmhouse Cider Cake

Evie's Pudding

Eve's Rhubarb, Apple and Ginger Snow

Greek Custard Tart

Carrot Cake

Devil's Food Cake with Baileys Buttercream

Chocolate Whip

Myleene's Quick Banana Pud

Tour Cookie Bake

Irish Chocolate Muffins

Strawberry and Coconut Cake

Marble Cake with Orange Drizzle Syrup

Hazelnut, Cherry and Amaretto Meringue Cake

Mary's Banana Bread

Phil's Mum's Fruit Cake

Pineapple Upside-down Puds

Coconut Polenta Cake with Honey Syrup and Berries

Raspberry Cream Melting Moments

Malteser Cake

Energy Balls

Welsh Cakes

Lebkuchen

Liquorice Allsort Slice

Lemon and Raspberry Brioche Bread and Butter Pudding

～～～～～～～～～～～～～～～～～～～～～～～～～～～～～～～～～～

In the past few years I have discovered and come to adore horse riding. Penny and her husband Lawson run Nolton Stables in Pembrokeshire, where you can ride their horses along the beach and through the woods. Riders of any ability can do this, and it's one of the best experiences I have ever had. Billie and I, and also John and his children, go whenever we can. Penny and Lawson have become friends and on our last visit they invited us to come over to their wonderful home for dinner. Penny made a brioche bread and butter pudding, which was so amazingly crispy on the top yet soft and buttery underneath that I pestered her for the recipe. She told me she did it all by sight, so I made one up. For Penny and all the Owens family, with all my love x

Serves 4-6

I x 300g brioche loaf,
   thickly sliced
50g unsalted butter, melted
100g lemon curd
2 medium eggs
50g caster sugar, plus
   extra for sprinkling
100ml double cream
400ml milk
300g raspberries

Heat the oven to 180°C/gas 4. Grease a 23 x 15cm baking dish.

Lightly toast the brioche slices, then cut into triangles and spread both sides with melted butter and a scraping of lemon curd.

In a bowl, whisk the eggs, sugar, cream and milk together and leave to stand for a few minutes.

Layer the triangles into the baking dish, overlapping them a little, then scatter with the raspberries and a little sprinkle of sugar if you wish. Pour over the cream mixture and bake in the oven for about 40 minutes until golden brown on top.

Chocolate and Coconut Torte

My sister's friend Amanda is a busy working mum but she manages to make really exciting lunches at the drop of a hat. Amanda made this torte for one of her impromptu lunches, then gave the recipe to Victoria after she kept on talking about it and how good it was! My sister doesn't usually get excited about cake, so this was one recipe I had to get my hands on. I have played with the recipe a little and used coconut oil instead of the original butter to give it a slightly different flavour dimension, and I have to say it's pretty darn good.

Serves 8-10

200g dark chocolate (about
   36 per cent cocoa solids;
   I use Bournville)
1 tbsp vanilla bean paste
140g coconut oil, melted
4 medium eggs
170g caster sugar
250g ground almonds
icing sugar, to dust

Heat the oven to 170°C/gas 3. Grease and line a 23cm round loose-bottomed cake tin with baking parchment.

Using a knife or food processor, chop the chocolate into tiny pieces. Stir the chocolate and vanilla paste into the melted coconut oil.

Put the eggs and sugar into a bowl or stand mixer and whisk for 8–10 minutes until the whisk leaves a ribbon on the surface when lifted. Fold in the chocolate coconut oil and almonds and pour into the cake tin. Bake in the oven for around 35 minutes until cooked through but still slightly gooey. Dust with icing sugar just before serving.

Farmhouse Cider Cake

I do a lot of work around food for my amazing friend Kate Thornton's website TBSeen.com, so inevitably we chat about recipes. This is Kate's mum's recipe, which she has kindly passed to me. It's quite a light-textured, crumbly cake, almost like a madeira cake with fruit in it, but the cider gives it a lovely apple-y flavour. A real old-school classic.

Serves 8-10

350g self-raising flour
pinch of salt
175g demerara sugar
175g unsalted butter
275g mixed dried fruit
grated zest of 1 orange
1 large egg, beaten
150ml dry or sweet cider
2 tbsp good-quality
   marmalade (any kind you
   like, with rind or without)

Heat the oven to 180°C/gas 4. Grease and line a 20cm round cake tin with baking parchment.

Sift the flour and salt into a mixing bowl, stir in the sugar and rub in the butter with your fingers until it resembles breadcrumbs. If you don't want to do this by hand, you can use a food processor.

Stir in the dried fruit and orange zest, then make a well in the centre and add the egg, cider and marmalade. Stir well and pour into the prepared cake tin.

Bake in the oven for 50 minutes, then lower the heat to 150°C/gas 2 and bake for a further 15 minutes or until a skewer inserted into the centre comes out clean. Leave to cool in the tin before slicing.

Evie's Pudding

Whatever life throws at us, I know Emma and I will always hold each other's hand. We have been best friends since we were 11 years old and she has always been there for me. Her daughter Evie is a joy and loves to bake, hence the play on the name for this traditional pudding that Emma and Evie make while preparing their Sunday dinner. They have it ready to go in the oven once everyone has sat down to enjoy their roast chicken!

Serves 6

4-5 cooking apples
pinch of cinnamon
2 tbsp soft light brown
   sugar
100g unsalted butter
100g golden caster sugar
2 medium eggs
100g self-raising flour
drop of vanilla extract
170g blackberries
custard, to serve

Heat the oven to 180°C/gas 4.

Core, peel and chop the apples, then place in a pan with the cinnamon and brown sugar and stew over a low heat until the apples are soft but still holding their shape.

Cream the butter and caster sugar together in a bowl, then beat in the eggs, flour and vanilla extract.

Place the stewed apples in the base of a shallow pie dish, add the blackberries then spoon over the cake mixture. Bake in the oven for 30 minutes, until the cake has cooked through and serve with custard.

Eve's Rhubarb, Apple and Ginger Snow

A beautiful and funny mum Eve told me she used to make this twist on the classic apple snow for her children, then one day decided to put dollops of cream on top and serve them as individual puddings at a dinner party. They went down a storm and she has made them ever since. I've used forced rhubarb, which makes them a lovely bright pink, but out of season you could replace the rhubarb with 100g of raspberries. This is a light and pretty pud. Please note that you have to eat it within a couple of hours of making it, otherwise the snow collapses.

Serves 8

3 large, tart apples
2 sticks of forced rhubarb, chopped
I knob of stem ginger
3 large egg whites
60g icing sugar
stem ginger syrup (optional)
shortbread thins, to serve

Core, peel and chop the apples and put them in a pan with the rhubarb. Add enough water to barely cover them, bring to the boil then reduce the heat and simmer gently until the apples and rhubarb are completely soft. Drain off any excess liquid then whiz the fruit with the ginger in a food processor until you have a smooth purée. Set aside to cool.

Beat the egg whites in a clean bowl until foamy. Then add the icing sugar, a little at a time, beating constantly until you have a firm, shiny meringue.

Beat in the apple and rhubarb purée a little at a time; the mixture will grow and become dense. Add more icing sugar or some stem ginger syrup if you want it a little sweeter. Serve with shortbread thins to dip in.

Greek Custard Tart

I love this recipe for *Galaktoboureko*, a Greek custard tart, from my sister's friend Maria. The recipe has been in Maria's family for years - her grandmother used to make it for tea parties and social gatherings, a tradition Maria and her mother continue today - and I feel very proud to be able to include it in my book. It looks a little like baklava because the crisp layers of filo pastry are drenched in a sticky syrup and then cut into the same shapes, but the nuts of baklava are replaced by a custard. All traditional custard recipes for this tart contain semolina, which gives it its characteristic grainy texture and also enables it to stand up well. I think it is absolutely delicious - unlike any other custard tarts you'll try - and I find the sticky sweetness very moreish.

Serves 8-10

I litre milk
3 medium eggs, plus 2 egg
  yolks
100g caster sugar
100g fine semolina
2 tsp vanilla extract
120g unsalted butter,
  melted, plus extra for
  greasing
225g filo pastry

For the syrup
150g caster sugar
2 tsp lemon juice
I tsp vanilla extract

Heat the oven to 190°C/gas 5. Brush a 23 x 30cm ovenproof dish or baking tin with melted butter.

Pour the milk into a pan and bring to just below boiling point, then remove from the heat and allow to cool slightly.

In a bowl, lightly beat the eggs, egg yolks and sugar together until thoroughly blended. Stir in the semolina. Transfer the mixture to a large heavy pan and pour in the hot milk, stirring constantly. Simmer over a low heat, still stirring, for about 10 minutes until smooth and thick. Remove from the heat, add the vanilla extract and 3-4 tablespoons of the melted butter.

Cut the filo sheets to fit the dish and spread half of them on the base, brushing each with melted butter before laying on the next. Pour in the custard and spread evenly over the filo.

Stack the remaining sheets on top of the custard, brushing each with melted butter before adding another layer. Using a knife, cut 4 strips lengthways into the pastry layers without cutting through the edges. Brush the top of the tart with butter and sprinkle with a little water. Bake for 15 minutes, then reduce the oven temperature to 160°C/gas 3 and bake for a further 35 minutes until the top is golden and crisp.

continued overleaf ···>

For the syrup, place the sugar and lemon juice into a pan, pour in 125ml water and bring to a boil, stirring until the sugar is dissolved. Boil without stirring for 7 minutes, then remove from the heat, stir in the vanilla extract and leave to stand for 10 minutes to thicken.

Spoon the syrup over the pastry as soon as it is out of the oven. Allow the pastry to cool and absorb the syrup, then cut into 5cm squares or diamonds and serve warm or at room temperature.

Carrot Cake

According to my friend Denise, her grandma made the best carrot cake. She would go round to her house and eat slice after slice and it is one of the memories she really associates with her grandma. I love that food can do that. I have such vivid recollections of my own grandma's rock cakes and whenever I make them I'm back in my Nanna's kitchen. Carrot cake is a classic and I don't believe in messing much with tradition, so this is my truly delicious carrot cake, designed to transport Denise back in time!

Serves 6-8

225ml sunflower oil
170g soft light brown sugar
3 medium eggs
1 tsp vanilla extract
2 tbsp maple syrup
juice of 1 small orange
300g self-raising flour
1 tsp baking powder
½ tsp mixed spice
250g carrots, grated
60g chopped walnuts

For the icing

300g cream cheese (take it
  out of the fridge a good
  hour before you use it to
  stop it splitting)
190g icing sugar
50g unsalted butter
2 tsp lemon juice

Heat the oven to 180°C/gas 4. Grease and line two 20cm cake tins with baking parchment.

In a stand mixer or with an electric hand whisk, beat together the oil and the sugar, then add the eggs one at a time, making sure each is fully incorporated. Continue to beat while you add the vanilla extract, maple syrup and orange juice.

Fold the flour, baking powder and spice into your wet mixture, then fold through the carrots and walnuts. Divide the mixture between the tins and bake for around 25-30 minutes until a skewer inserted into the centre comes out clean. Leave to cool in their tins for 10 minutes before transferring to a wire rack.

While the cakes are cooling, beat together all the ingredients for the icing, then spread half on the bottom layer of the cake, sandwich the two halves together, then spread the remaining icing on top.

Devil's Food Cake with Baileys Buttercream

In the wake of *MasterChef* I feel so fortunate to have made some really good friends from doing food shows, and Jo Wheatley is one of them. Jo won *The Great British Bake Off* in 2011, and her cakes are second to none. Every recipe I have ever tried of hers works perfectly, and her book is always on my kitchen table. She has taught me how to ice cakes and given me lots of great tips. I know it might be considered a bit retro, but for me a devil's food cake is just the best chocolate cake, and Jo's is my absolute go-to recipe. I have made it so many times and it's the one I'm always asked to make for birthdays. I've sandwiched her cake with a Baileys buttercream so it's definitely one for the grown-ups, however you can just leave the Baileys out if you want to bake it for a child's birthday. Don't be put off by the coffee in this cake; you honestly can't taste it, it just adds to the richness of flavour. Enjoy with a cup of tea and a friend!

Serves 10-12

250g caster sugar
250g self-raising flour
1 tsp baking powder
1 tsp bicarbonate of soda
60g cocoa powder
3 medium eggs
150ml whole milk
150ml sunflower oil
1 shot of espresso coffee,
   topped up with 100ml
   boiling water

For the Baileys buttercream

500g unsalted butter at
   room temperature, cubed
1kg icing sugar, sieved
1 tsp vanilla extract
1-2 tbsp Baileys, depending
   on taste (optional)

Heat the oven to 170°C/gas 3.

In a large bowl, mix all of the dry ingredients together. In a separate bowl or jug, mix the eggs, milk and oil together. Pour the wet ingredients into the dry and stir to combine, then gradually stir in the coffee.

Divide the mixture between three 20cm sandwich tins and bake in the oven for 25 minutes, or until a skewer inserted into the centre comes out clean. Leave to cool for 5 minutes in their tins, then turn out and cool on wire racks.

For the icing, whip the butter in a stand mixer or food processor for about 7 minutes until pale and almost double the size. Add the icing sugar gradually, beating well after each addition. Add the vanilla extract and mix well, then with the machine running, very slowly drizzle in the Baileys, if using.

Take a piping bag fitted with a star nozzle and fill it with the icing. Pipe rings on to the bottom layer of the cake, then top with the second layer, pipe again, top with the final layer and pipe again. Leave to firm up in the fridge for 30 minutes and serve.

Chocolate Whip

I think we all have memories of puddings we ate as children. Food, like music, has the power to transport me back to when I was five, sitting at my grandma's kitchen table. One of my strongest memories is trying to get the last bit of chocolate whip out of the bowl with my fingers because it was the best thing I had ever tasted, the sun shining in through the window and making a line of light that looked like a light sabre. This is that pudding (with thanks to my mate Gav for the memories and for the chocolate whip!). If you're making these for children, leave out the brandy.

Serves 6

125g dark chocolate (about
   36 per cent cocoa solids;
   I use Bournville)
4 medium eggs, separated
I tsp hot water
I tsp vanilla extract
I2g unsalted butter
I tbsp brandy (optional)
I00ml double cream

Melt the chocolate in a heatproof bowl set over a pan of barely simmering water, then set aside to cool a little.

With an electric hand whisk, beat the egg yolks, water, vanilla extract, butter and melted chocolate, then fold in the brandy, if using.

Beat the egg whites in a clean bowl until they hold stiff peaks. Gently fold the egg whites into the chocolate mixture, being careful not to knock out the air. Spoon into pretty glasses or a large serving bowl and chill in the fridge for at least 2 hours.

Whip the cream until stiff, then transfer to a piping bag fitted with a star nozzle. Pipe little stars on top (or whatever pattern you fancy).

Myleene's Quick Banana Pud

My friend Myleene Klass is the first person to say that she is not a cook, but this Filipino dish is one that her mother taught her and she now makes it for her own daughters. It's naughty but really nice, and if I'm feeling very indulgent I'll let Billie spread Nutella over the base of her wrapper before folding it around the banana. If you can't get the pancake wrappers, filo pastry works just as well.

Makes 8

vegetable oil
4 bananas
4 sheets of filo pastry
8 tsp soft light brown sugar
icing sugar, to serve
vanilla ice cream, to serve

Cut the bananas in half crossways. Place 1 sheet of filo on the worktop and cut it in half lengthways. Place a banana piece in the bottom third of each strip before sprinkling with 1 teaspoon of sugar and rolling up, tucking the ends in as you go. Repeat with the remaining ingredients.

Heat 3cm of oil in a deep pan over a medium heat until it is shimmering and hot.

Using tongs, gently lower the wrapped bananas into the oil and cook for around 4 minutes, turning regularly, until brown and crispy. Serve with a dusting of icing sugar and vanilla ice cream.

Tour Cookie Bake

My mum's cousin Jane was a ballet dancer for years. She is Canadian and now has her own dance school in Vancouver. When she was touring, Jane used to make batches of these cookies to give her a quick energy boost on the road. I've kept her original recipe but just use whatever dried fruit you have in the cupboard.

Makes about I2

180g plain flour
40g wholemeal flour
½ tsp bicarbonate of soda
good grating of nutmeg
I tsp salt
175g unsalted butter
170g soft light brown sugar
I tsp vanilla extract
I egg
2 medium bananas, mashed
200g rolled oats
50g desiccated coconut
90g raisins (or use dried
   cranberries, blueberries,
   etc)
I00g dark chocolate chips

Heat the oven to 180°C/gas 4. Grease and line a 20 x 30cm brownie tin with baking parchment.

Sift the flours, bicarbonate of soda, nutmeg and salt into a bowl.

In another bowl, beat the butter and sugar until really light and fluffy, then add the vanilla extract and the egg and beat well. Add the bananas, oats, coconut, raisins and chocolate chips and stir to combine. Pour the wet ingredients into the dry ingredients and mix well.

Spread the mixture out in the brownie tin and bake for 20–25 minutes until golden brown. Cut into squares or bars in the tin and allow to cool for 10 minutes before transferring to a wire rack to cool completely.

Irish Chocolate Muffins

Noleen used to produce *This Morning* and was the person in my ear when I was presenting. She's Irish so on St Patrick's Day she made these delicious muffins. I love that they look like little pints of Guinness. You can't really taste the Guinness – it just gives the muffins a richer flavour. Noleen told me her kids, hubby and in-laws find these hard to resist and I can see why.

Makes 16

250ml Guinness
250g unsalted butter
80g cocoa powder
400g caster sugar
2 medium eggs
1 tsp vanilla extract
150ml soured cream
300g plain flour
2 tsp bicarbonate of soda
½ tsp baking powder

For the icing
150g unsalted butter
300g icing sugar
75ml soured cream

Heat the oven to 180°C/gas 4. Line two 12-hole muffin tins with 16 cases.

Heat the Guinness and butter in a pan over a medium heat until the butter is melted – don't let it boil. Lower the heat and stir in the cocoa powder and sugar until you have a rich, dark, shiny liquid, then remove from the heat.

In a large bowl or stand mixer, whisk the eggs, vanilla extract and soured cream until combined, then stir in the warm Guinness liquid.

Mix the flour, bicarbonate of soda and baking powder together in a bowl. Then gradually add to the Guinness mixture, beating well.

Fill each muffin case with mixture until two-thirds full. If you fill them too high, when the muffins rise they will spill out over the sides and stick together.

Place in the oven for 20-25 minutes – they are ready when a skewer or cocktail stick inserted into the centre comes out dry. Remove from the oven and allow to cool a little before taking the muffins out of the tin and placing them on a cooling rack. They will still be very soft so try and hold them near the top of the muffin case so as not to squish them.

For the icing, beat together the butter and icing sugar in a bowl until smooth and thick, then stir through the soured cream. When the muffins are cool, use a small spatula or flat butter knife to ice each one. If you ice them when they are too warm the icing will melt and slump.

Strawberry and Coconut Cake

My friend Nicola's daughter Abby is an amazing, creative baker. She bakes when she is happy and when she needs to feel happy. By seven years old she was a better baker than Nicola - although by her own admission Nicola can burn water! Nicola says she watches Abby in the kitchen and it makes her so proud. I have made this many times now for cake sales and tea parties and it's always gone in 60 seconds.

Serves 8-10

200g caster sugar
225g unsalted butter
3 medium eggs, beaten
200g self-raising flour,
    plus extra for dusting
40g unsweetened desiccated
    coconut
400g strawberries
1-2 tbsp milk
coconut flakes, to decorate

For the icing
300ml double cream
1 tsp vanilla extract
1 tbsp icing sugar, plus
    extra for dusting

Heat the oven to 180°C/gas 4. Grease and line two 18cm round cake tins with baking parchment.

In a stand mixer or with an electric hand whisk, beat the sugar and butter together until light and fluffy, then continue to beat while you add the eggs a little at a time. Add the flour and desiccated coconut and fold in until everything is combined.

Take 300g strawberries and dab them with a kitchen towel to remove any moisture. Chop the strawberries finely and dust with flour. This prevents them from sinking to the bottom of the cake. Fold the strawberries into the cake mixture, divide the mixture between the tins and bake in the oven for 20-25 minutes, until a skewer inserted into the centre comes out clean.

While the cakes are baking, whisk the cream, vanilla and icing sugar in a bowl until thickened. Slice all but a few of the remaining strawberries thinly. Remove the cakes from the oven and turn them out of the tins. Leave to cool on a wire rack.

Once cooled, sandwich the cakes with the cream and sliced strawberries. Decorate the top of the cake with coconut flakes and the reserved whole strawberries, then dust with icing sugar.

Marble Cake with Orange Drizzle Syrup

To be honest I have always found marble cake a little dry so it's never been up there on my list of cakes to turn to. However, this one from my friend Andri has changed my mind. It's the oil that keeps hers really moist. I've also discovered that marble cake is a fun one to make with Billie because she loves swirling the batter. I've added an orange drizzle syrup which goes so well with the chocolate and leaves a lovely glaze.

Serves 8-10

60ml sunflower oil
300g caster sugar
4 medium eggs
420g self-raising flour
170ml milk
2 tsp baking powder
1 tsp vanilla extract
70g dark chocolate chips
2 tbsp cocoa powder

For the syrup
grated zest and juice of
 2 oranges
6 tbsp caster sugar

Heat the oven to 160°C/gas 3. Grease and flour a 1.5-litre Bundt tin.

In a bowl, whisk the oil, sugar and eggs together. Sift the flour into a separate bowl, add the oil mixture then add 20ml of the milk, the baking powder and vanilla essence and stir to combine.

Pour half the mixture into the tin and stir the chocolate chips into this. Add the cocoa powder and the remaining milk to the mixture still in the bowl and mix well, then pour the chocolate mixture on top of the vanilla. Using a knife, make swirls through the mixture to create a marble effect.

Bake in the oven for 45 minutes, or until a skewer inserted into the centre comes out clean, then remove from the oven and cool in the tin for 15 minutes before turning out on to a wire rack.

Meanwhile, make the syrup by placing the orange juice and zest in a pan with the sugar and 3 tablespoons of water. Bring to the boil and leave to bubble away until it is thick and coats the back of a spoon.

Make holes in the top of the cake. Pour over half the syrup while the cake is still warm and allow it to be soaked up. Once cool, transfer to a serving plate and just before serving pour over the remaining syrup.

Hazelnut, Cherry and Amaretto Meringue Cake

There is something magical about hazelnut meringue as it has all the delicious taste of a classic meringue, but with an added nuttiness and chewiness that just leaves me wanting more. Cherries are my favourite fruit (I take after my granddad, who would choose them over any dessert) and the amaretto cream just tops it off. I think it's a great alternative to the more traditional options at Christmas - perfection in a pudding.

Serves 6-8

5 medium egg whites
250g caster sugar
I tsp cornflour
I tsp white vinegar
I tsp vanilla extract
I00g toasted hazelnuts,
    chopped

For the filling
400ml double cream
I tbsp icing sugar
2 vanilla pods, seeds
    scraped
I tbsp amaretto
400g pitted cherries
    (tinned or fresh), halved,
    plus about 25 whole
    cherries to decorate

Heat the oven to 140°C/gas 1. Line 2 baking sheets with baking parchment and draw a 23cm circle on to each piece of parchment.

In a clean bowl, whisk the egg whites until stiff peaks form, then add the caster sugar in a steady stream while still whisking the whites. Once they go glossy, fold in the cornflour, vinegar and vanilla extract, then slowly fold in the toasted hazelnuts.

Scoop half the mixture on to each circle and spread out as evenly as possible. Bake in the oven for 1-2 hours, until you can start to peel the baking paper away from the meringue easily, then turn off the heat and leave the meringues to sit in the oven until cool. This will help prevent the meringue cracking.

For the filling, whisk the cream with the icing sugar and vanilla seeds until soft peaks form, then stir in the amaretto.

Spread half the cream over one of the meringue bases. Scatter with the halved cherries, then spread most of the remaining cream on the underside of the other base and place on top of the cherries. Dot the underside of the whole cherries with cream and use this to stick them to the top of the cake to decorate.

Mary's Banana Bread

My friend Mary is responsible for the super popular strawberry and almond Fantasy Cake in my first book. She is a fantastic baker, mother and actress. It's funny because when I was talking to people about this book, almost everyone I knew had a banana bread recipe for me, but I knew that if there was one to try it was Mary's. I have thrown different fruits in, and used coconut oil as the fat, and – as ever – Mary's cake is a joy.

Serves 8-10

280g wholemeal flour
2 tsp baking powder
2 tsp bicarbonate of soda
I tsp salt
I tsp cinnamon
I tsp mixed spice
3 medium bananas
I tsp vanilla paste
150ml almond or coconut
   milk (in a carton)
150ml maple syrup
115ml coconut oil, melted
50g dark chocolate, chopped

Heat the oven to 160°C/gas 3. Lightly grease a 450g loaf tin.

Mix all the dry ingredients together in a bowl. In a separate bowl, mash the banana with the vanilla paste. In a third bowl, combine the milk with the maple syrup and coconut oil.

Stir the milk and syrup mixture into the dry ingredients, then add the mashed banana and chocolate. Mix well and pour into the loaf tin. Bake for 40-50 minutes until a skewer inserted into the centre comes out clean.

Phil's Mum's Fruit Cake

The chef Phil Vickery is someone I am really proud to call a friend. We have done food shows together and put the world to rights on many an occasion. Phil has told me several times how, despite the fact that you train to be a chef and they teach you all this stuff, some of the most useful things he has learned are from his mum. When I told him about my book, he said that his mum's boiled fruit cake is one of the best he has ever baked. Boiling the fruit makes the cake really moist – it is definitely among the best ever.

Serves 8-10

450g mixed dried fruit (I prefer more sultanas than any other fruit)

50g chopped natural glacé cherries

225g unsalted butter, cut into small cubes, plus extra melted butter for greasing

250ml cold water

250g golden caster sugar

2 large eggs, beaten

290g self-raising flour, sifted

1 tsp bicarbonate of soda

2 tsp mixed spice

2 tbsp black treacle

Place the dried fruit, cherries, butter, water and sugar into a large stainless steel pan and bring to the boil. Boil for 5 minutes, stirring occasionally, then remove from the heat, cover and leave until cold.

Heat the oven to 180°C/gas 4. Line an 8cm deep, 25cm square cake tin with 2 layers of baking parchment and brush with melted butter then dust with a little flour.

Place the cold fruit mixture into a large bowl. Add the eggs, flour, bicarbonate of soda, mixed spice and black treacle, mix well and place in the prepared baking tin.

Place in the oven and bake for about 75 minutes until well risen and dark brown. If the cake browns a little too quickly, cover it loosely with a piece of foil for the remaining cooking time. Remove from the oven and leave to cool in the tin completely before slicing.

Pineapple Upside-down Puds

I know school dinners aren't exactly high on everybody's list of meals they remember fondly, but I used to love school puddings. This was one of my favourites when I was little and the smell of it baking in the oven brings back memories of walking through the school hall in the morning, smelling this cake and seeing the dinner ladies write it on the board. I would run back and tell everyone in my class that it was 'pineapple upside-down cake for pudding!' I've made my own version a lot less stodgy than the school's, as well as making them individual puddings, and they still delight me every time I eat them.

Makes 12-14

275g golden syrup
12 canned pineapple rings
  in natural juice, drained
12-14 glacé cherries
275g unsalted butter, plus
  extra for greasing
275g caster sugar
275g self-raising flour
1 tsp baking powder
4 large eggs
100ml milk
2 tsp vanilla extract
custard, to serve

Heat the oven to 180°C/gas 4.

Grease 12-14 125ml ramekins or dariole moulds and place a circle of baking parchment on the base of each dish. Divide the golden syrup between the dishes, then place a pineapple ring into each (chop the pineapple rings if the base isn't big enough for a whole ring). Place a glacé cherry in the middle of each pineapple ring.

Place the butter, sugar, flour and baking powder in the bowl of a food processor. In a separate bowl, lightly beat the eggs, milk and vanilla extract together and pour into the processor bowl. Blitz for 1 minute until thoroughly blended (you could also do this by hand or with an electric whisk).

Spoon the mixture into the ramekins and level out with a palette knife. Bake for 20 minutes until golden and a skewer inserted into the sponge comes out clean. Leave to cool in the ramekins for 15 minutes. Turn out on to individual plates and serve warm with custard.

Coconut Polenta Cake with Honey Syrup and Berries

‑‑‑ ‑‑‑

I made this cake up one spring day when I was meant to be writing this book. I always find the beginning of the writing process pretty hard and will find anything to do except sit at my laptop! I wanted to make a cake that could be served warm as a pudding as those are my favourite. This one also happens to be gluten-free, though that wasn't my intention when I made it. The cake is delicious and moist and the honey syrup with the berries really works. I have made this again and again for friends and family and, without fail, everyone loves it.

Serves 8-10

140g coconut oil
120ml maple syrup
4 medium eggs
200g ground almonds
100g polenta
2 tsp baking powder
grated zest and juice of
    1 lemon
2 tbsp milk (I use coconut)
125g runny honey
few drops of orange blossom
    water (optional)
400g raspberries and
    blueberries
crème fraîche or natural
    yoghurt, to serve (optional)

Heat the oven to 180°C/gas 4. Grease and line a 23cm cake tin with baking parchment.

In a stand mixer or with an electric hand whisk, beat together the coconut oil and maple syrup, then whisk in the eggs one at a time. Stir in the almonds, polenta, baking powder, lemon zest and juice and the milk and pour into the prepared tin. Bake for 40-50 minutes, until a skewer inserted into the centre comes out clean.

When the cake has just come out of the oven, heat the honey and 60ml water in a pan until warmed through and just starting to simmer, then add a few drops of orange blossom water, if using. Skewer the cake so there are lots of holes in it, then pour the honey syrup all over it. Leave to cool in the tin.

Remove from the tin, top with the berries and a good dollop of crème fraîche or natural yoghurt, if using, and serve.

Raspberry Cream Melting Moments

Melting moments are crumbly, buttery Australian biscuits, typically sandwiched with raspberry cream, that I fell in love with when I first went over there. The biscuits are so crumbly and soft they really do just melt in your mouth. Traditionally, the raw biscuits are pressed with a fork to mark out the indent, but you could just use your thumb print for a slightly less dainty finish. John told me that his family made them this way when he was a child - that's how they all knew which melting moments were theirs.

Makes 18-24

250g salted butter
75g icing sugar
I tsp vanilla extract
240g plain flour
70g cornflour

For the filling
100g raspberries
½ tbsp icing sugar
300ml double cream

Heat the oven to 160°C/gas 3. Line 2 baking trays with baking parchment.

Beat the butter, icing sugar and vanilla extract together in a bowl until light and fluffy, then stir in the flour and cornflour until you have a soft, buttery dough (try not to handle it too much).

Flour your hands, take a teaspoon of the dough and roll it into a ball. Place it on one of the lined baking trays, then repeat with the remaining dough, leaving a couple of centimetres between each one on the baking trays. Flatten them with a fork to make an indentation (or use your thumb, if you prefer).

Place the trays in the fridge for a good 15-30 minutes.

Put the raspberries in a pan with the icing sugar and cook over a low heat until they break down. Sieve to remove the seeds, then allow to cool. Whip the cream until it is just starting to thicken, then swirl through the cooled raspberry purée.

Bake the melting moments for around 15 minutes, then leave them on the baking trays for 5 minutes before transferring to a wire rack to cool. When completely cooled, sandwich the biscuits together with the raspberry cream.

Malteser Cake

I met Gill Hornby on a coach in Dubai on our way to a festival of literature. Gill was sat behind me (with her friend Eve, who gave me the rhubarb and apple snow recipe on page 177) and saved me during a two-hour traffic jam as we chatted about our lives and the books we had written. I told her about the idea behind this book and she offered to send me the recipe for her Malteser cake. When I got home I bought her novel *The Hive,* which is about motherhood and female friendships, and read it pretty much in one sitting. The Malteser cake features in Gill's book and I feel honoured that she very kindly let me include it in mine.

Serves IO

I x 38g tube Smarties
85g unsalted butter
2 tbsp golden syrup
7Og milk chocolate
35g dark chocolate
I tbsp cocoa powder
200g plain digestive
    biscuits
200g Maltesers
edible gold spray, to
    decorate

Line a 450g loaf tin with cling film, then scatter a layer of Smarties over the base of the tin.

In a pan, melt the butter with the syrup, milk and dark chocolate, then stir in the cocoa powder and remove from the heat.

Crush the biscuits and half the Maltesers into small pieces (make sure you don't turn everything to dust). Add to the chocolate mixture with the whole Maltesers and the remaining Smarties and stir to combine.

Press the mixture into the loaf tin and place in the fridge for 2 hours to set. When ready, invert the tin on to a serving plate and lift the tin off. Peel away the cling film, then have fun playing with the edible gold spray to decorate it, before slicing.

Energy Balls

My friend Jane has recently got into making healthy energy balls for her family, and because we often discuss food I decided to give hers a go. I've discovered that when I'm running into a yoga class after working all day and need a quick, energising snack beforehand these always do the trick. Recently I made a batch to take to Billie's sports day for the mums to snack on, but the girls kept sneaking over and eating them. In fact Billie said, 'Mamma, you must put these in your book as we all love them.' High praise indeed.

Makes 18

200g pitted dates
200g ground almonds
4 tbsp cocoa powder
4 tbsp coconut oil
desiccated coconut, for
   dusting

Chop the dates in a food processor until fine, then add all the other ingredients except the desiccated coconut and process again until the mixture is combined and sticks together.

Place the desiccated coconut in a shallow bowl. Take 1 heaped teaspoon of the mixture and roll it into a ball then lightly coat in the desiccated coconut. Repeat until all the mixture is used up. Chill in the fridge for 30 minutes to set.

Welsh Cakes

I filmed a great little series for *This Morning* called 'Coastal Cottage'. We were in Pembrokeshire and went to Hilton Court, one of the most beautiful places I have ever been. It has magnificent gardens and a fabulous tearoom. Heidi, who works there, taught me how to make Welsh cakes. She has to make hundreds as they fly out of the kitchen, and until now the recipe has been a family secret – but she has very kindly allowed me to use it in the book. These are absolutely delicious served warm with lashings of butter. I've substituted the traditional raisins with sour cherries, only because I'm not a big fan of raisins, but you could stick with tradition if you prefer.

Makes 12

250g self-raising flour
½ tsp baking powder
120g unsalted butter, plus
  extra for greasing
75g caster sugar, plus
  extra for sprinkling
75g dried sour cherries
1 medium egg
1-2 tbsp milk

Sift the flour and baking powder into a bowl. Rub in the butter to form breadcrumbs then stir in the sugar and dried cherries.

In a bowl, beat the egg with the milk then pour into the breadcrumb mix. Stir to form a dough.

Lightly dust a work surface with flour and roll the dough out to 5mm thick. Cut out rounds with a 7.5cm cutter, re-roll the trimmings and cut out more cakes.

Place a flat griddle pan or large heavy-based frying pan over a low-medium heat. Once hot, grease it with a little butter or oil. Cook the Welsh cakes in batches for 3-4 minutes on each side, adjusting the heat if necessary so they are golden brown on the outside and cooked right through.

Remove from the pan, sprinkle with caster sugar and serve immediately.

Lebkuchen

Meredith is my sister's best friend. She is very proud of the fact that her grandmother was German and she embraces all things Germanic. Lebkuchen are spiced biscuits, a bit like soft gingerbread but coated in a thin glacé icing and chocolate, traditionally eaten at Christmas. Meredith's version is chewy and moreish, and I love the fact that she told me she melted leftover Easter bunnies for the chocolate coating, something I often do too as Billie soon forgets about her Easter hoard.

Makes about 20

100g runny honey
100g black treacle
175g dark brown soft sugar
1 medium egg
grated zest of 1 lemon, plus
   a squeeze of juice
350g plain flour
½ tsp bicarbonate of soda
generous pinch of ground
   cloves
3 tsp ground allspice
30g ground almonds
30g finely chopped
   hazelnuts
200g milk chocolate

For the icing
200g caster sugar
2 tbsp icing sugar

In a medium saucepan over a medium heat, stir together the honey and treacle. Bring the mixture to a boil, remove from the heat and stir in the brown sugar, egg, lemon zest and juice.

In a large bowl, stir together the flour, bicarbonate of soda, cloves and allspice. Add the treacle mixture to the dry ingredients and mix well. Stir in the almonds and hazelnuts and bring together to form a dough. Cover and chill in the fridge overnight.

Heat the oven to 180°C/gas 4 and grease 2 baking trays.

Using a small amount of dough, roll out on a lightly floured surface to 5mm thick. Cut out shapes such as stars or hearts and place on the baking trays. Re-roll any trimmings and cut out more shapes. Bake for 10 minutes until no imprint remains when lightly touched. Cool on a wire rack.

Meanwhile, for the icing, combine the caster sugar and 100ml water in a small saucepan. Heat to between 110°C and 115°C on a thermometer, or until a small amount dropped into cold water forms a soft ball that flattens when removed from the water and placed on a flat surface. Remove from the heat and stir in the icing sugar. Brush the icing over the biscuits while they are still hot. If the icing becomes grainy, re-heat slightly, adding a little water until the crystals dissolve.

Melt the chocolate in a heatproof bowl set over a pan of barely simmering water. Spread on the bottom of the biscuits or dip them into it. Leave to set.

Liquorice Allsort Slice

John's sister-in-law Jane and I have become really close and it's always great to catch up with them in Australia, even if it's usually a flying visit! Jane makes this slice for her children who are great strapping teenagers but still love being looked after by their mum. It's definitely one for those with a sweet tooth, but delicious in small quantities and really great for a children's party.

Makes 20

185g unsalted butter, plus
  extra for greasing
1 x 397g can condensed milk
1½ tbsp golden syrup
375g Digestive biscuits,
  crushed to a fine crumb
80g desiccated coconut
400g liquorice allsorts,
  coarsely chopped
300g milk chocolate,
  chopped
30g coconut oil

Grease and line a 22 x 28cm baking tin or dish with baking parchment.

Combine the butter, condensed milk and golden syrup in a pan over a low heat. Cook, stirring continually, for 5 minutes or until the butter has melted and the mixture is smooth.

Pour into a large heatproof bowl, add the crushed biscuits, coconut and liquorice allsorts and stir until just combined.

Press the mixture into the base of the prepared tin and leave in the fridge for 30 minutes to set.

Place the chocolate and coconut oil in a heatproof bowl over a pan of barely simmering water. Use a metal spoon to stir until the chocolate has melted and the mixture is smooth. Pour the melted chocolate over the slice.

Place in the fridge for 1 hour to set, then cut into 3cm squares to serve.

MYLEENE KLASS

Quick Banana Pud

JANE WACE

Tour Cookie Bake

NOLEEN GOLDING

Irish Chocolate Muffins

ANDRI LANITIS

Marble Cake with Orange
Drizzle Syrup

KATE THORNTON

Farmhouse Cider Cake

EMMA DE SOUZA

Evie's Pudding

MARY MCCOY

Banana Bread

GILL HORNBY

Malteser Cake

TESS & PHIL VICKERY

Fruit Cake

EVE WHITE

**Rhubarb, Apple &
Ginger Snow**

JO WHEATLEY

**Devil's Food Cake with
Baileys Buttercream**

HEIDI FOSTER

Welsh Cakes

MEREDITH HEPNER CHAPMAN

Lebkuchen

JANE TYLER

Energy Balls

AMANDA BANNISTER

Chocolate and
Coconut Torte

GAV AVISON

Chocolate Whip

NICOLA SHINDLER

Strawberry &
Coconut Cake

PENNY OWENS

Lemon & Raspberry Brioche
Bread & Butter Pudding

DENISE VAN OUTEN

Carrot Cake

JANE LAWLER

Liquorice Allsort Slice

MARIA VLACHOS

Greek Custard Tart

INDEX

* * * * * * *

Acknowledgements

* * * * * * * * * * * * * * * * * *

My thank yous have to start with all the amazing women
– my friends and friends of friends (including a few men!)
who gave me their recipes and were happy to let me change
and play with them and make them my own. These recipes
are now out in there in the world for even more people to
enjoy, so thank you so much for sharing.

Thank you to my fantastic editor Imogen, whom I have been
wanting to work with for a long time. Finally I got you and
my instinct was right – you are brilliant.

To Lizzie, my pixie, my home ec, food stylist and my friend.
One day I'd like to be you!

To the A-Team who worked on creating this book: my now
friend and super clever photographer Chris Terry, his
assistant Danny, Lizzie's assistant Katie Marshall, stylist
Olivia Wardle, designer David Eldridge and my wonder-
woman make-up artist Justine Ward.

To everyone at Simon and Schuster, especially Ian,
Suzanne and Nicki.

To Jonny, my agent and friend, and to Laura Carson and Jonathan Conway.

To my John… Always… All ways, a million thank yous.

To my sister Victoria, my inspiration as a mother; I learn from you every day.

To my daddy, for all your advice and wisdom and never-ending love and support.

To my mummy for making me; and my Billie for making me a mummy.

The publishers and Lisa would like to thank Sytch Farm Studios for the loan of their plates, bowls and serving dishes for the photography, and DeVol Kitchens.

******

For every mother,
however she came to be.

First published in Great Britain by Simon & Schuster UK Ltd, 2017
A CBS company

1 3 5 7 9 10 8 6 4 2

Simon & Schuster UK Ltd
1st Floor
222 Gray's Inn Road
London WC1X 8HB

www.simonandschuster.co.uk
www.simonandschuster.com.au
www.simonandschuster.co.in

Simon & Schuster Australia,
Sydney

Simon & Schuster India,
New Delhi

A CIP catalogue record for this book is available from the British Library

Hardback ISBN: 978-1-4711-2562-1
eBook ISBN: 978-1-4711-6085-1

Colour reproduction by Aylesbury Studios Ltd, UK
Printed and bound by LEGO in Italy

Design and art direction: Two Associates
Photography: Chris Terry
Food styling: Lizzie Kamenetzky
Prop styling: Olivia Wardle
Hair and make-up: Justine Wade
Project editor: Imogen Fortes
Copy editor: Rachel Malig

The Turkey Schnitzel and Chik Chak Salad recipe on page 34 is taken from Emma Spitzer's
book *Fress*, and is used with permission from Mitchell Beazley.